Glenn Alterman's

SECRETS TO SUCCESSFUL
COLD READINGS

Glenn Alterman's

SECRETS TO SUCCESSFUL

COLD READINGS

BY GLENN ALTERMAN

CAREER DEVELOPMENT SERIES

Smith and Kraus, Inc.
Hanover, New Hampshire

Published by Smith and Kraus, Inc.
177 Lyme Road, Hanover, NH 03755
www.SmithandKraus.com

First Edition: July 2007
10 9 8 7 6 5 4 3 2 1

Cover design and book production by Julia Gignoux, Freedom Hill Design
Cover photo by Ashton Worthington
Text design and formatting by Kate Mueller, Electric Dragon Productions

ISBN 1067-134X
ISBN 978-1-57525-566-8
Library of Congress Control Number: 2007930049

THE AUTHOR

GLENN ALTERMAN is the author of *The Perfect Audition Monologue, Sixty Seconds to Shine: 101 Original One-Minute Monologues, Street Talk, Uptown, Two Minutes and Under (volumes 1, 2, and 3), The Job Book: One Hundred Acting Jobs for Actors, The Job Book 2: One Hundred Day Jobs for Actors, What to Give Your Agent for Christmas, Two-Minute Monologues, Promoting Your Acting Career, Creating Your Own Monologue,* and *An Actor's Guide: Making It in New York.*

Two Minutes and Under, Street Talk, Uptown, Creating Your Own Monologue, The Job Book (1 and 2), and *An Actor's Guide: Making It in New York City* were all "Featured Selections" in the Doubleday Book Club (Fireside Theater and Stage and Screen Division). Most of his published works have gone on to multiple printings.

He wrote the book for *Heartstrings: The National Tour* (commissioned by the Design Industries Foundation for AIDS), a thirty-five city tour that starred Michelle Pfeiffer, Ron Silver, Christopher Reeve, Susan Sarandon, Marlo Thomas, and Sandy Duncan (among others).

His plays have been performed at Primary Stages, Circle in the Square Downtown, the Turnip Festival, HERE, LaMama, the Duplex, and Playwrights Horizons, as well as at many other theaters around the country.

Alterman's play *The Sealing of Ceil* recently won the prestigious Arts and Letters Prize in Drama. His play *Nobody's Flood* won the Bloomington National Playwriting Competition as well as being a finalist in the Key West Playwriting Competition. *Coulda-Woulda-Shoulda* won the Three Genres Playwriting Competition three consecutive times (including publication of the play in three separate editions of the Prentice-Hall college textbook). It has received several productions around the country. *Spilt Milk* received its premiere at the Beverly Hills Rep/Theater 40 in Los Angeles and was twice selected to participate in the Samuel French One-Act Festival; it's had over twenty productions. *The Danger of Strangers* won Honorable Mention in both the Deep South Writers Conference Competition and the Pittsburgh New Works Festival and was a finalist in the George R. Kernodle Contest. There have been over fifteen productions of it, including Circle Rep Lab and the West Bank Downstairs Theater Bar, starring *The Soprano*'s James Gandolfini.

His plays *Like Family* and *The Pecking Order* were optioned by Red Eye Films (with Alterman writing the screenplay). His play *Solace* was produced Off-Broadway by Circle East Theater Company and presently has several European productions. *Solace* was recently optioned for European television. Other plays include *Kiss Me When It's Over* (commissioned by E. Weissman Productions), starring and directed by Andre DeShields; *Tourists of the Mindfield* (finalist in the L. Arnold Weissberger Playwriting Competition at New Dramatists); and *Street Talk/Uptown* (based on his monologue books), produced at the West Coast Ensemble. *Goin' Round on Rock Solid Ground, Unfamiliar Faces,* and *Words Unspoken* were all finalists at the Actor's Theater of Louisville.

He is one of the country's foremost monologue and audition coaches, having helped thousands of actors in their search for (and preparation of) monologues for auditions, as well as developing cold-reading skills for auditions. He recently was voted first runner-up as "the best private acting coach in New York" by the readers of *Backstage* newspaper.

Alterman has lectured and taught at such diverse places as the Edward Albee Theater Conference (Valdez, Alaska), Southampton College, Governors School for the Arts (Old Dominion University), the School for Film and Television, Western Connecticut State College, Broadway Artists Alliance, the School for Professional Actors, Star Map Acting School of Long Island, the Dramatists Guild, the Learning Annex, the Screen Actors Guild, the Seminar Center, and in the Boston public school system, as well as at many acting schools and colleges all over the country.

In 1994 he created The Glenn Alterman Studio (www.glenn alterman.com) and through its auspices has worked privately as a monologue/audition coach and at colleges, universities, and acting schools all around the country.

Alterman presently lives in New York City where he coaches actors; writes plays, books, and screenplays; and acts in TV commercials and film. He can presently be seen in an American Airlines commerical opposite James Gandolfini.

This book is dedicated to my students,
past and present.

They say that by your students you're taught.

Well—I've learned a great deal.

Thank you all very much!

CONTENTS

ACKNOWLEDGMENTS

I'd like to sincerely thank all the casting directors, playwrights, and actors who accepted my phone calls and agreed to participate in this book. Their advice, opinions, and insights are truly the "secrets" of this book.

Usage Note: For consistency, the pronoun *he* is used throughout the book whenever a *he* or *she* might be used. This is done for expediency and clarity. Hopefully, this will not alienate or offend anyone of either sex. The author is aware that to some this might seem politically incorrect and apologizes to anyone offended.

INTRODUCTION

When I began work on this book, I wasn't aware of how important cold-reading skills are to an actor's career (and craft). I soon discovered, however, that the actor who has limited cold-reading skills is really at a great disadvantage when auditioning. Almost all auditions, especially commercial auditions, include cold reads. In theater and film auditions, an actor can be called in to read for a role and, if not right for that role, will be often be asked to read for another role. In these situations, he's generally given very little time to read over the new material, thus the cold read. Returning to the audition room, he is expected to have an understanding of the new material and to have made specific acting choices. If he has good cold-reading skills and delivers a knockout second audition, he may actually land the job.

As I learned what it takes to give a good cold reading, I realized that it actually goes hand and hand with being a good actor. Being able to trust your instincts, be in the moment, and go fully with personalized choices are important to auditioning, rehearsing, and performing.

I recently saw Al Pacino on the TV show *Inside the Actors Studio*. He spoke about how invaluable his first impression of a script is when he works on new material. Much of how he develops his characters comes from that first impression. That first impression is an actor's gut reaction to new material. It's what you must learn to rely on at cold readings.

This book deals with all areas of acting where cold-reading skills are required: plays, television, film, monologues, TV commercials, and voice-overs. I've interviewed the top casting directors in all fields and asked what I felt were the most pertinent questions regarding cold readings (and auditions in general).

I think you'll find, as I did, that many of their replies and insights were not always what I expected. Aside from the interviews, I've also included dozens of insights from many New York– and Los Angeles–based casting directors and actors.

My hope is that every actor who reads this book will walk away with a total understanding of how to successfully cold read new material for his audition and, hopefully, book jobs. But this is not just a book on cold readings. There's a great deal of information here on the best ways to prepare and give all auditions.

My goal in writing this book was to write the consummate book on cold readings. I've approached this subject from every angle and offer not only advice but working examples and exercise material for you to work with.

I've also included many seldom-done monologues that you can use at your next audition where monologues are required.

I'd like to thank all the actors who have written to me over the years to express their appreciation of my previous books; it means a great deal to me. I hope you find this book to be useful for all your auditions.

Best of luck,
Glenn Alterman

10 WAYS TO GET THE MOST OUT OF THIS BOOK

1. This book is written for the actor who is familiar with cold-reading skills as well as the actor who is just learning how to develop those skills. To get the most out of this book, I suggest that you don't read the book from cover to cover.

2. I think you should first read "48 Basic Requirements for All Cold Readings" and "25 Technical Rules for All Cold Readings." These chapters lay the foundation for all the chapters that follow.

3. Next, look through the contents and see what stands out for you—those areas that interest you. For instance, if you're presently auditioning exclusively for commercials, you may want to go to that chapter next, followed by the chapter where I interviewed TV commercial casting directors. If you're primarily a theater, TV, and film actor, go to those chapters first, and don't forget to read the casting director interviews that follow.

4. After you've read through the chapters that interest you most, I suggest that you *then* read through the entire book, taking notes or highlighting those things that you find may apply to your career.

5. Pay particular attention to the analysis sections. I believe you'll find these sections especially helpful and informative. Learning how to analyze a script in a short period of time and make personalized choices is key to all auditions.

6. Once you've started practicing the cold-reading advice in this book at auditions, see how you're doing. If you'd like to improve, refer to the appropriate chapters and exercises.

7. If you have some auditions coming up for daytime television or film, you may want to reread the chapters with interviews of casting directors before going to those auditions. I've interviewed the top casting directors in those fields.

8. Once you've finished reading the book, put the information you've learned into practical use. Go out there, audition, and see if your cold-reading and auditioning skills have improved. This is not a theoretical book; it's a practical one. The goal is to help actors get jobs.

9. Don't feel you need to apply every rule in this book. Depending on where you are in your acting career, some guidelines may not be pertinent to the way you work. If something you've learned before reading this book regarding cold reads still works for you, continue using it. If it's not broke, you don't need to fix it. But always leave room for discovering new ways to work, things that you can add to what has worked in the past.

10. Whenever you feel the need, refer to the book and review the material until it becomes second nature. There's a lot of information in this book; it may take a while to apply everything you learn.

My purpose in writing this book was not only to instruct but to inspire. Once you develop confidence in any skill, fears can be alleviated. With any audition, there is always some tension, some apprehension: that's only normal, accept it. But I believe that by learning how to overcome that fear (with knowledge, insight, and practice), you'll find that you may start to enjoy auditioning.

Chapter 1

WHAT IS A COLD READING?

I look to see if the actor has a clear understanding of the character. I want to see strong, intelligent choices. Do they understand the context of the scene? Actors don't need to bring in props for the audition. Also, don't work on a lot of blocking; it's unnecessary. Some actors think if they fumble over a few lines, they've blown the audition. The words are the least important part.

**Marc Hirschfeld, casting director,
executive vice president, Casting, NBC**

asically a cold-read audition is auditioning new material with a script in hand. You may have been given the sides (pages from the script) an hour ago or just ten minutes ago. In any case, there isn't a great deal of time for you to prepare. There is what some call the "freezing cold read," which is when you are just handed material and asked to read it at the audition without getting a chance to read through it first.

If the cold reading is from a play, you generally will not have time to read the entire play. You're expected to quickly read through the material you've been given, make choices, and come back into the audition room and give a (hopefully) good audition. Cold readings occur in TV commercial auditions, as well as in theater, film, and TV auditions.

WHY WE NEED TO KNOW HOW TO COLD READ MATERIAL

Actors need to work. Cold readings are one of the ways in which you can get a job. Let's say you've come in to read for a character in a play or movie. You've worked hard, prepared the material you were previously given, and read for the casting team. They like what you've done with the material but feel that there's another character in the play or movie that you might be better suited for. Great. At that point they'll hand you the sides for the new character and tell you to go out "and take a look at the new scene." You're expected to peruse the material, understand it, make specific, personal choices, and then come back into the audition room and show 'em what you got. You're being given another shot. This is not a rare occurrence; it happens all the time.

With commercials, you're generally not given the material until you show up at the audition. There is no at-home preparation. You get a copy of the material, have a few minutes to make some choices, and then in you go and your audition begins. You're expected to make the material fly. You're expected to have made specific choices. You're expected to commit to the choices you've made. Sometimes these auditions can lead to booking a national spot that can make you many thousands of dollars and give you great exposure.

THE ARTISTIC VALUE OF DEVELOPING COLD-READING SKILLS

Whenever I coach an actor, I always give him new monologue material and tell him to read it cold. We're talking really cold here. The actor doesn't have time to read through the material, not even once. I want actors working with me to learn to fly by the seat of their pants, to trust their instincts. I want them to make instant choices. I want my students to realize that they have the ability to make strong, personal choices in the moment. I want them to learn to be spontaneous. Some actors love this challenge; others become fearful. Many actors underestimate how smart they really are. But more important, many actors just don't trust their instincts. To me, much of acting is really about just that—trusting your instincts and going with it.

ENCOURAGING SPONTANEITY

Sometimes great moments occur purely by chance. Perhaps you've had the experience of being in the audience when an accident occurs onstage during a production of a play. Suddenly, adrenaline shoots through the cast as well as through the audience. Perhaps a glass broke onstage, and now everyone in the cast needs to be spontaneous in his reaction to the broken glass. I actually saw this happen once during a play when the two actors onstage had no shoes on and a bottle of wine broke. The audience sat up in apprehension. The apprehension grew when yet another cast member came onstage barefooted, perhaps unaware of the broken bottle. The scene took on a heightened sense of real danger. Everything turned out OK. The lesson here: Accidents can sometimes be great in creating exciting spontaneity onstage. Spontaneity is something actors always want to include in their performance. It makes their work alive, vibrant.

MEETING THE COLD-READING CHALLENGE: ONE STORY

I remember working with Andre DeShields on a production of my play *Kiss Me When It's Over*. The play was a series of dramatic and comedic monologues. Andre was directing. He asked all the actors to sit in the same room. Then one by one, he would give an actor a new monologue to read cold—freezing cold. They would then sit and audition in front of all the other actors. For many, I'm sure, it was a frightening experience. But those who went with their gut, took a chance, allowed their intelligence and talent to shine, got callbacks and, in some cases, got the job.

WHAT THE CASTING TEAM EXPECTS FROM ACTORS DURING A COLD-READING AUDITION

There's no two ways about it: What the casting team really hopes for is a great performance. They want to believe that you're the right one for the role. I know it sounds ridiculous, given the time you're usually given to prepare, but they expect "magic." And I have seen magic occur at many cold-reading auditions. It has to do with how much an actor honestly believes in what he is doing—connecting to the material and committing to it. Bottom line, if you believe, they'll believe. If you put your insecurities out there, they'll see them too. And just so you know, there is a perceivable difference between faking confidence and really believing in what you're doing.

Always take over your audition, make it your own. And by this, I don't mean in a pushy, phony way, but in a sincere, professional way. Confidence is paramount to giving a good audition.

If it's a monologue audition, don't ask questions like: "Do you want me to use you?," referring to where you should be looking, or "Is it OK if I stand?" If you need to ask those questions, you haven't made specific choices as to whom you're talking to (in your imaginary world) before starting the audition.

The answer to the question "Do you want me to use you?" is no. Never "use them" unless they specifically ask you to. Occasionally, an agent will ask you to use him because he wants to get a sense of how you read on camera. In that situation, it's OK to use the agent.

Whether you stand or sit depends on the moment in the play that the monologue takes place. The material always dictates whether you stand or sit.

JUDGING THE AUDITION MATERIAL

When it comes to the script, you must believe in it fully. If you waste your preparation time judging how poorly written it is, or how your character is not fully developed, you run the risk of sabotaging your audition. I'm not saying you have to be in total denial about a bad script or an underdeveloped character, but just make whatever is there on the page work for you. Creative actors can make bad writing work by making strong choices that fill out the holes in the script. You're not a dramaturge; you're an actor. You're job is to interpret, to make what's on the page work. If you really feel the material is second rate, you can always find some excuse to turn down the role in the event that you get it.

I don't care if you're playing the worst mass murderer ever, you must always find the positive in every character you play. You must empathize and even love the character you're auditioning for. You must discover, in the little time you have to prepare, what motivates him to say or do the things he does. You must take his side. The world's worst villains all believe they have a noble purpose. You must find what motivates your character. As soon as you judge your character to be the "bad" guy, you start to detach. In their minds, many so-called villains believe that they are saints, people with a noble purpose, getting revenge for something they felt unjustly punished for. You must try to rally to your character's cause with your personal choices. If you don't, you'll slide into caricature or melodrama.

I look for actors who are listening to their auditioning partners or to the reader. A big don't for me is actors who have the words so memorized that it's all mechanical. They wait a specific amount of time before they respond, etc. It's all too rehearsed, too planned, not spontaneous or in the moment. I like to read with actors because they're paying attention to what I'm saying. And if I take a beat between a certain line reading and they've jumped over my words, it's because they're so rehearsed in it. Nerves, particularly by the time they get to a network, is something that we have to take into consideration.

I always look for previous work that the actor has done that I can show to the executives if I feel that his audition didn't come off well. If I've seen that actor in a film project or in TV or theater and he doesn't hit it in the room, I'll do everything I can to help him. With those actors whose work I know and who don't audition well, I try to come to bat for them with the executives by saying things like, "This actor just doesn't audition well. Listen to the voice. Does the height work for you? Does the age work for you? Physically is he the right type? You're not going to see it in the audition. I know this actor's work, though." A lot of actors look at the audition as a work in progress. There's an immediacy about television. The time from when an audition takes place to when a role needs to be cast to getting the show on the air is so small. Some- times wonderful actors need to speed up the process that they'd usually take. At an audition where an actor might just be getting comfortable in the idea of what the role is, he's expected to give a finished performance. But the re- ality of doing television means actors are constantly given new pages just minutes before they're about to shoot the scene.

Peter Golden, executive vice president,
Talent and Casting, NBC

Chapter 2

48 BASIC REQUIREMENTS FOR ALL COLD READINGS

If I'm reading a script, I get a feeling about the characters. The reason that people hire us is we follow the script, and we try to find who the characters are and match that with the right actor. There are times when someone comes in that isn't what we thought the character would look like, but the actor makes the role his own. I did that with Haley Joel Osmont for The Sixth Sense.

Sometimes you'll say to a director "I know that this isn't what you're looking for, but look what he did." Those kinds of surprises can be really great, as can when an actor who hasn't done much acting comes in, auditions, does a good job, and ends up getting a break.

Avy Kaufman, casting director

These are the must-dos for all cold-reading auditions. Hopefully, if you learn and use these rules, you'll ace many of your auditions.

1. You should develop the habit of reading things cold every day at home. It doesn't make a difference if it's a play, a poem, newspaper copy—anything. Just pick it up and

read it absolutely cold. Quickly try to find the essence of what the material is about. Get used to reading cold. It's a muscle that can be developed.

2. If at the audition you are offered the opportunity to take more time to read over the material or come in and just read it cold, *always* go for more time. Sometimes actor's nerves makes an actor think he can just "wing it." That's a risk you shouldn't take if you don't have to. The more time you have with the material, the better you can understand it and make strong, personal choices.

3. Always try to get to your audition as early as possible. Because you don't have the material in advance, you'll need to spend more time. Generally at a cold-read audition, I suggest arriving at least a half hour earlier than your audition. Obviously, the more time you have the better.

4. When you arrive at the audition, read the material very carefully. Mine it for every nugget of insight that you can use. Analyzing the material, really understanding it, is the first step to making strong, personal choices. Try to figure out what the script is about. What is the playwright trying to say? What is the relationship between your character and the other character(s) in the scene? Get a sense of what you're feeling in the scene. Try to understand the world of the play, the mood of the scene. The underlying thoughts, the subtext of the character, are what you're really looking for.

5. Sometimes the sides may include material from the scene before yours and/or the scene after yours. Read this material, too, as it may give you important insights into the character you're auditioning for.

6. Your nerves can hinder your ability to peruse the material. Calm yourself, breathe, relax. The more thoroughly you

can read the material, the better. Your first impression is very important, always trust it.

7. You are always looking for information in the script that will inspire you to make actable, personalized choices. Once you understand what motivates the character you'll be playing, see if you can identify with his situation.

8. Don't intellectualize the material. Some actors overanalyze material. Make it simple; don't get bogged down in details.

9. Don't underestimate your first reaction. Trust your instincts and go with what you've got! You must feel confident in what you do at the cold reading. Believe in your choices and commit to them fully. Your first impression, that first read, can give you everything you need (if you read carefully). Actors sometime second-guess their first impressions. Don't. An audition is the worst time to second-guess what you feel is right.

10. If you have time to reread the material and find something that you may have missed in the first read, add this new information to what you have. The more information you have about your character, the scene, and the play, the better.

11. If it's a long piece, break it down so that you can work on it section by section. Break it down into beats or segments. If a sentence is very long, break it into sections.

Immediately focus on the given circumstances in the scene. Understanding and making decisions based on the given circumstances are the king pins to all auditions. Throughout this book, I'll be calling your attention to the use of the given circumstances with all types of material. The given circumstances are:

- What is this scene about? Try to discover the world that this play or scene takes place in. What is the event? What is the story of the scene(s) you're auditioning for.

- Who is the character? You should get a feel for the character that you're playing. If you don't, you'll just be reading words from a script at your audition. The bottom line on auditioning and acting in general is that you must create a fully alive character. You need to understand your character and identify with him. Look for information about his intelligence, his class, his philosophy, his feelings (particularly his feelings for the other character[s] in the scene), his predicament. See where you can connect with him; use your imagination.

- What is the relationship between your character and the other character(s)? You must always determine what the relationship is between your character and the person you're talking to. Do you like, love, or hate this person? Do you need him for something? Even if it's a monologue, you must decide on what the relationship is between the imaginary person and your character. Why are you talking to him?

- Where is the character? Determine where the scene takes place. If it's not mentioned in the script, then use your imagination. Locale can affect a character's emotional state. A man in a prison cell will behave differently than a man at work in an office.

- Does this scene take place in the present, past, or future? What time of year is it? What time of day or night? Again, these factors may contribute to the way you play your character.

- What is the character doing? Find playable actions that you can perform at the audition. Be careful not to bog yourself down with too many actions. Make it simple.

- What does he want? You must have a strong intention for every scene you audition for. The intention is the driving force of the scene. It's the need, the goal, of your character. You can act verbs, not nouns. It's better to do things that the character would do, than trying to just be the character. Always try to choose a strong intention for every scene you audition for. Pick an active verb, something that can bring you to actively participate in the scene. It all comes down to what does your character want in that scene and how will he go about getting it.

- What is preventing your character from getting what he wants? What is the obstacle? Knowing and playing the intention and finding and playing the conflict is crucial to any scene. Obstacles come in all forms— from a character's insecurities or neuroses to the other character in the scene doing something that prevents you from getting what you want. Bottom line: whatever impedes you from getting to your goal is the obstacle that your character is trying to overcome.

- What's at stake? The urgency in the scene comes out of how driven and focused your character is and how much he wants something. Audition scenes that lack urgency are generally not very exciting. The more "life and death" your situation is, the more driven your intention will be, and the scene will be more passionate. Pick strong active intentions and play them, and you'll have an engaging audition.

12. Once you've decided on your intention and objective, try to keep to it in your audition. Don't give up your intention because of something the other actor does at the audition. I'm not suggesting that you shouldn't play off what the other actor is giving you; just maintain your intention.

13. If you can't get answers from the text itself, use your imagination and create what you need to make the material your own. Imagine your character's history and back story. Try to be truthful to what you see in the sides; don't just make up a past that has no connection to the story on the page. Having a history for your character is a way to deepen what's already there on the page. It allows your imagination to fill in blanks that might not be there in the script.

    One way to create your character's history is to observe what other characters in the scene say about your character. Don't just concentrate on the facts in his history. You want to create a history that emotionally connects you to him. I realize that at a cold-reading audition, you don't have much time to prepare. Imagining your character's history is time-consuming and should only be worked on *after* you're sure what the given circumstances are, especially your intention in the scene.

14. Personalizing is integral to connecting you to the character and a better audition. You are the character that you're reading for; the character is you. Start off saying the words as yourself. If there's enough time, paraphrase what's on the page. Find ways to identify with the character.

15. Actors sometimes preoccupy themselves too much with the style of the scene rather than their truth in the scene. Style plays a part, but who your character is (as you see

him) is what's really important. You can always work on the style in rehearsal if you book the job.

16. Try to make your choices as simple as possible. Because you're given such little time, you're better off making simple, playable choices rather than elaborate, complex ones.

17. When working on the scene before the audition, rehearse at about 75 percent; save some for the actual audition. Go off into a corner somewhere, find a hallway, or perhaps rehearse in the bathroom. You want to get a sense of how the scene will feel when you actually say the lines out loud at the audition. Obviously, if it's a very emotional, nervous breakdown scene, you can't pull all the stops out in the audition area.

18. Playwrights and screenwriters have specific ideas about the characters in their plays. Quite often, they include what the character is feeling or doing at a certain moment. This is true more often with screenplays. You should read the writer's ideas in the script, take them to heart, and then decide whether you want to play them out fully or not. Some actors totally disregard what the playwright says in his stage directions. Some actors like to play the opposite of what is obvious in the text. This is risky, but it can work. It depends on how open the creative team is to your interpretation. What they will appreciate, however, is that you have made a specific choice and are committed to it. They can always give you an adjustment.

19. Always notice the playwright's use of punctuation in the script. Punctuation can give you clues as to the way your character breathes his words and sentences. It may inform you of the rhythms of the scene you're auditioning for.

20. See where the beats are, where transitions occur. One thing you always want to show in an audition is variety.

You don't want to be playing the same note throughout. Be aware of emotional shifts that occur in the scene. Some actors mistakenly latch on to one emotion that they discovered at the beginning of a scene, and that's all they play, even if the material suggests others. They notice, for instance, that their character starts the scene off crying or is angry and then play the entire scene in tears or having a tirade.

21. As far as emotions go at an audition, don't go running after them or try to force them. The best way to create honest emotions is to create the conditions from which they organically arise. There is some amount of trust necessary when it comes to having genuine emotions during an audition or in performance. You have to trust that if you've done your work beforehand, they'll happen. Understanding the circumstances and playing the actions are key.

22. If you're honestly reacting to the other actor at the audition, you may find yourself surprised by unexpected emotions that come up in the moment. Try to remain open to what you're given in the scene. Spontaneity, acting in the moment, is a big plus at an audition.

23. Don't try to second guess what "they (the casting team) are looking for." It's a waste of time. Sometimes casting team members think they know what they're looking for, but then someone walks in and changes their minds.

I know from my own experience that when an actor walks in to audition for me and makes the part his own, it's hard not to give him real consideration, even if he's far from what I had in mind. A good example of this was when we were casting my play *The Danger of Strangers*. It's an erotic thriller. I wanted the man to be stunningly handsome and sexy and the woman to be a knockout. When James Gandolfini and Susan Aston auditioned for the roles, my mind was totally switched around. They didn't physically fit the description: not that they're bad looking, but they just weren't what I had in mind. But they're damn good actors, and they made the parts their own. Needless to say, they got the job.

24. Cold reading isn't just about reading words from a page and pretending to feel; it's about creating a real flesh-and-blood character in the moment. Some actors think that just "coloring" words or phrases, pretending to feel, indicating emotions, is enough for an audition. You really have to be willing to dance on the edge of the sword, expose yourself.

25. If there is a surprise in the scene, your character (you) should honestly react to it. Since we rarely know exactly what other people are going to say in life, we are always being surprised to some degree. This is true of characters in plays too.

26. Always read and try to understand the other character's lines in your scene. Reading only your lines over and over in the waiting area may get you stuck in a by-rote pattern of line readings. You want to understand where the other character is coming from.

27. Don't let the critical voices in your head overcome your focus. We all have judgmental voices criticizing our work. Nowhere is it more detrimental than when we're auditioning. Focus on the material, your intention, and your character and not those dreaded self-doubting voices.

28. Most actors rush their readings. Don't let your nerves speed you along during the read or the actual audition. Breathe, don't forget to breathe! *Stay in the moment!* Stay in control of the dialogue; don't rush it. You don't want to leave the audition with regrets.

29. Use all your senses to keep you connected to your character's emotional world. Most actors just use only one or two of their senses; indulge yourself.

30. As part of your preparation, always have a prebeat before you start the audition scene. Prebeats help you focus on the material so that you're not too distracted or stressed out by the audition itself. Most actors start their auditions too slowly because they didn't have a strong prebeat. They tentatively wade into the water of the scene. Focus your attention on what has occurred the moment before the scene actually begins and use that as a launchpad to say your first line. Because auditors see so many actors for a role, they have a very short attention span. If you aren't there in your first couple of lines, you may lose them.

31. Make sure to make eye contact with the other person that you're reading with. Whether it's another actor or the casting director, stay connected with him. That's not the same as staring nonstop into his eyes as if you were in a trance. In real life, we look into people's eyes for a bit, then look away for a moment, and then reconnect again. Only insecure actors do the locked eyeball-to-eyeball thing.

32. Use your imagination. It's a mistake to just keep to what's on the page. Allow yourself to imagine what it would feel like if this were really happening to you. The more you can immerse yourself in the imaginary world, the more successful your audition will be. Remember the magic "as if."

33. Even if the other actor isn't doing a good job, or if the stage manager is reading and giving you nothing, stay in the moment as your character. You must create the impression that he is truly the other person in the scene. Listen to what the other character is saying.

34. Your relationship with the other character(s) in the scene is key to making a cold read work. You are not flying solo here. It's about how you respond to what the other character has just said and how that impacts on you. It's one of the given circumstances that is so key. Without the relationship in the scene, you're just an actor flying solo, disconnected. *Relationship! Relationship! Relationship!*

35. Say the lines as "you" in the imaginary situation. Sometimes actors mistakenly try to make the character talk as another person; it doesn't really come from themselves. The problem with doing this is that you may end up with a caricature rather than a character.

36. Use substitution whenever you need to. Obviously, we won't be able to relate to every scenario we come across at an audition. Feel free to use something from your own life to connect to the material. Substitution is one way that you can understand where your character is coming from, his emotional life.

37. Feel free to break up the line. Don't feel compelled to read sentence after sentence after sentence. Reading like that is not lifelike. Only actors give line readings in complete sentences. In life we may pause during a sentence, reflect in the middle of a line (or word), or have an emotional response midphrase. Modulate.

38. Your honest reaction in a comedic scene can make or break the comedic moment. Don't try to play the jokes or what's funny to you as the character. The character doesn't think it's funny. Quite often the character is having a hell of a time—that's what makes it funny.

39. I'm sure you've heard this before, but it's worth repeating: If your character in the scene is inebriated, don't play

drunk. Resist "showing drunk," and go for what the character needs.

40. Even if the script calls for you to be smoking a cigarette, chewing gum, or be drinking a beverage—don't. All you have to do is indicate these things (minimally). Bringing in props to your audition can be distracting and generally is a waste of time.

41. Some actors have a tendency to look at their next line in the script while the other character is speaking. How you listen is being observed by the director and casting director just as much as when you speak. This is especially true in film and TV auditions.

42. Enjoy yourself! Acting is an enjoyable experience. Actors sometimes look terribly strained, anxious, stressed out. All acting really is, is make-believe. Remember when you were a child and played with your dolls or soldiers, sometimes for hours? You were just having fun, living in your own private fantasy world. Unfortunately as we get older, we're told by adults to stop pretending, to grow up. That wonderful world of imagination that we had as children atrophies. The good news is that as actors we can reawaken the wonderful imaginary world that lives in all of us. *Have fun!*

43. Do it for you. Those actors who spend much of their energy in trying to please the casting director or director, lose out on what's really important here—doing it for yourself!

44. You must be available for any adjustments that the director or casting director may give you after you've done your reading. Yes, you are given high marks for making strong choices, but sometimes your choices may not be

what the director had in mind for the scene or the play. You must be flexible and willing to take the adjustments the director suggests. Sometimes he'll ask you to add to what you've just shown them. And sometimes he'll want to take the material in a whole new direction. You must be willing to change course at a moment's notice. It may not be what you had in mind. It may not be even something you feel about the character, but you must at least attempt to meet his request. Sometimes a director will purposely ask you to make an adjustment just to see if you can take direction. An audition is not the time to challenge a director's interpretation.

45. Whether your scene includes a lot of dialogue for you or just a few lines, you still want to give it your all. Size does not matter; commitment, focus, and honesty do.

46. No matter what you do, do it with total conviction at the audition. That doesn't mean overact. It means do it fully, from your heart. You don't want to leave the audition room saying I could have done it better, why did I hold back?

47. Feel free to improvise within the text. Sometimes that opens a scene up for actors. I'm not saying add words or sentences, but if you feel comfortable, improvise with what's on the page.

48. If you honestly feel that you've totally strayed from the audition while reading, that you've lost your focus, you have the right to request that you start over again. You can only request this if you haven't been reading for too long, however. If you're on the fourth or fifth page, it's generally too late; they have other actors to see, and you're asking for too much of their time. A good rule of

thumb is not to ask to start over past the first page or two. If you make this request, be brief and quickly start again. Try to be more focused, more committed, on the second go-round; when an actor starts over again and gives the same (or worse read), it's annoying to the casting team. But don't overobligate yourself to blow them away. This isn't about trying to please them.

The most important thing you must remember is that casting directors are looking for a quality—not a performance. Be creative. Sean Penn, when he auditioned for the movie Taps, *showed us something entirely different, something that wasn't on the page. We can read, we know what the script says.*

It's the actor who's daring and comes in with something above what's on the page and makes fully committed choices. Of course, I must see an actor who can relate to the character. Just to go out on a limb is not enough if you don't know the inside of the character on the page. You must be able to expand what is on the page, enlarge it.

Shirley Rich, casting director

Chapter 3

25 TECHNICAL RULES
FOR ALL COLD READINGS

You look to see if the actor has a sense of the project they're auditioning for. During the audition, you're looking for the actor who can perform this role, has all the emotional colors necessary to do this part. The actor who takes that audition scene and can make it as colorful as the whole two-hour play or movie is a real find.

Bernard Telsey, casting director, Telsey+ Company

1. Be sure that you're warmed up before you enter the audition room. Actors sometimes arrive late and don't have enough time to relax and get ready to work. You should know the best way for you to warm up before an audition. Tension is the enemy. Obviously you can't start doing yoga or push-ups in the waiting area. Hopefully, you've done that (if you need to) before the audition.

2. Allow for extra time if you've never been to a new audition space. You want to feel comfortable in the waiting area and know your way around the audition space. You want to know where the bathroom is, where there is a

water fountain, and so on. In general, the more you know at any audition, the less nervous you'll be.

3. Don't socialize with other actors at the audition area. If someone wants to talk with you, tell him that you're preparing and that you can meet after for coffee or a chat.

4. Never keep your head buried in the script, forgetting to look up. Quite often an actor forgets to look up, and all we see is the top of his head. Many actors sabotage their good work by hiding their face in the page. All the emotion and energy that you may be feeling is going right back into the script, not out to your audience where it should be going. They want to see your eyes, what you're feeling. They can't see that with your head in the script. This is especially bad at on-camera auditions.

5. To avoid the habit of always looking down at the script, you may want to practice this exercise, "Taking a Sip of Word":

   • Look down at the script, get a line or two in your mind.

   • Then look up and say (send) the lines to the other person. Allow these lines to affect you so that you emotionally express what you (the character) is feeling.

   • Next look down at the next lines, then look up and send them, again expressing what you feel about the lines' meaning.

   • To keep your place in the script, allow your thumb to move down the side of the page as you progress. If you lose your place for a moment, it's totally OK, just find where you left off and continue. Losing your place in an audition may not even be noticed by those watching you. Stay in character until you find your place.

Don't beat yourself up for the rest of your audition just because of a momentary pause. This is not a paid performance, it's a cold-read audition. If you've ever watched a professional ice skater take a fall on the ice during a performance, you would have noticed that he immediately got right back up and continued with the routine as if nothing had happened. He finished the routine, bowed, and left the ice as if nothing bad had happened. This is exactly how you should audition after a flub.

- Relax, and try to do this in a natural up and down way. Focus your line reading to that other person (the spot you've picked).

6. It's been said many times that a great deal of acting is re-acting. Sanford Meisner, the acting teacher, taught that re-acting is key to all truthful acting. He felt that staying out of your head and being connected to the other actor(s) in the moment in the scene is key. The same can be said of an actor at an audition. Always allow the other actor's performance to be part of your audition. Listen, really listen, to what he's saying and react as honestly as you can.

   Actors often ask, "What if the actor I'm auditioning with is a terrible actor?" The best you can do is listen to what he (the character) is saying and react to it as best you can. You shouldn't spend too much of your audition time appraising the acting ability of the actor you're auditioning with. Your focus should be on playing your character as honestly as you can, and that also means reacting to whatever you're getting from the other actor.

7. Many casting directors suggest that you commit the first line of the script to memory. That way we won't be seeing the top of your head as you start the audition. Always

keep in mind that the first and last lines of any audition are very important: The first line because it's how they first see you doing the material and the last line because it's how you leave them.

8. Always place yourself in a position where you are looking forward as much as possible. If you're reading with the stage manager, he should be facing you with his back to the audience. The casting directors are not interested in his performance, but yours. If you're reading with another actor, try not to profile your face too much. Let them see as much of your face as possible.

9. Use the fourth wall as a way of letting them see the work that you're doing. Don't be afraid to look forward when the character is in thought. Many actors mistakenly look down at the floor when they're thinking or reacting.

10. Hold the script in your "off" hand. That is, if you're a righty, hold it in your left hand and vice versa. The idea is to not make your holding of the script too big a deal.

11. You don't want to use the script as a prop in the scene, waving it around, and so on. The more you downplay the script, the better.

12. Don't hold the script too high (covers your face) or too low (you have to look down at it). Hold the script about chest high.

13. Make sure they can hear you! Many actors speak too softly so they can't be heard. This is especially true in theater auditions. In film auditions, you can be more intimate, but you can't mumble your words and expect the camera to help you out. Something you should do on a regular basis is read out loud. Adjust the volume of your voice to the room you're reading (auditioning) in. Often actors read far too loud for a small audition space or can't

be heard in larger spaces, such as theaters. You must be understood and you must be heard!

14. Be careful about upward inflections at the end of your sentences. Actors, when nervous, will sometimes end their sentences with an upward inflection, which makes their sentences sound like questions rather than statements. Make sure that there is a period at the end of every one of your sentences

15. Practice reading difficult texts. I advise my students to read playwrights such as Shakespeare or Marlowe and even passages from the Bible on a regular basis (not specifically for religious purposes, unless they want to). You'll notice that over time you'll start to feel more comfortable reading complex material.

16. Accents are tricky things at auditions. I generally recommend that you don't attempt them unless they demand them at the audition. Nothing can take the auditors out of the auditions quicker than an actor who is going in and out of an accent. It's an unnecessary handicap. At a cold reading, you generally don't have the time to work on the accent during your preparation, so it shouldn't be expected.

17. Don't use the cold-read audition to improve or correct your acting based on criticisms you've received from acting teachers or critics of your work. Some actors try to correct acting problems during the audition. They recall comments about their acting or their speech and focus on correcting them at the audition, rather than focusing on the character and the imaginary world of the scene. They start to overpronounce words or artificially make their voice louder or try not to overact. A cold-read audition is not the time to correct bad acting habits.

18. Some actors can't decide whether to sit or stand during an audition. My advice is that unless you have a specific reason to stand, remain seated. In general, the material dictates the decision whether to sit or stand. If it's a very active scene, then being seated would not be appropriate. Actors standing without any real reason to stand tend to become self-conscious. But find a hard chair to sit on: soft, pillowy couches that swallow you up tend to sap your actor energy.

19. If you have found a genuine reason to stand during the cold read (for example, the text cries out for you to be up), feel free to use the space. Don't stay locked in one stance. If you feel the impulse to move, do so. That's not saying that you should fly all over the stage during the scene. Be prudent, but feel free to suggest what your character is doing.

20. Even if you're seated, try to express the character's physical life. Often I'll see an actor seated during a very emotional scene, crying, perhaps even yelling, with his legs crossed in a very relaxed manner. The lower half of his body is totally disconnected from the upper half. It's quite bizarre to see all that emotion happening from the neck up. Many actors become "talking heads" at their auditions.

21. Never place imaginary characters in the scene behind you, forcing you to turn your back to the casting director during the audition. Many actors unknowingly sabotage their auditions by talking to characters upstage. Place the other characters downstage so that we can see what's going on in your eyes.

22. Always make specific choices about your character. Actors occasionally make general choices about their character. The more specific you can be the better.

23. If you are dyslexic, you should tell the casting director or director at the start of the audition. They will interpret some of the pauses as actor/character choices. It's no great shame to be dyslexic, but it would be sad to lose getting a role because you weren't upfront about it. You'll need a little more time to read through the script. Let them know that.

24. Never apologize for your audition if you don't feel it went well. They may be satisfied enough to call you back. Generally actors are harder on themselves then casting directors. At the end of your audition, don't ask, "Was that what you were looking for?"

25. No matter how the audition went, never leave without smiling and saying good-bye to the auditors. Perhaps because of nerves, some actors practically run out of the room without saying "Nice to have met you" or even a simple thank you to the casting team. It's also OK to say good luck, but don't attempt to become their best friends. Be polite, be professional, be courteous. Leave the room confidently.

The actor's look is an important factor. I just need to believe the actor in the part, the character that he's reading for. It doesn't have to be the overall best reading, as long as the actor hits certain notes and I can believe him in the role of that character.

Louis DiGiamo, casting director

Chapter 4

25 COMMON
COLD-READING MISTAKES

I want actors to be good. I look for the actor who knows what he's doing, is professional. You want to feel the actor knows what the material is about. I really hate when an actor comes in, is introduced to the director, and seems befuddled. It's a profession, a business. A lot of young actors just think it's art.

Pat McCorkle, casting director

1. Actors, sometimes looking ahead in the script, don't react to what has just been said to them. Other actors artificially react to what's been said. In that case, you're in your head and not in the moment. Generally, you'll react a beat too late. I know that with nerves, "just being" can be difficult, but you must attempt to stay focused and in the moment.

2. It's no big deal if you mispronounce a word in the script. Actors sometimes get stressed out because they didn't pronounce that medical term or that foreign word in the script correctly. Do not backtrack and correct yourself; that only calls more attention to the fact that you've

blown the word. Think about it: In our daily lives, we all mispronounce words, so why can't your character? If you get the part, you can find out the correct pronunciation.

If there's a word in the script whose pronunciation really baffles you, ask the director before the audition how the word is pronounced. If you forgot to ask the director, then just say the word the way you feel it sounds. If it's a character's name that is difficult to say, again, ask the director how you pronounce the name.

3. One mistake actors often make in cold readings is biting off more than they can chew. It may be a long run-on line, and before you know it, you're in the middle of the line and feel you're just spouting words without any meaning. Long, complex sentences often require you to break them into bite-size, palatable pieces so that you know what you're saying.

4. Don't just say the words on the page. Think while speaking. Think in character when auditioning. This is a character in a play, not just words to be expressed with a general emotion. Use yourself, your emotions, and your life as the palette to create the character.

5. Try not to play just the quality of the character but play how he'd express that particular quality.

6. Don't let your energy run down during an audition. Some actors run out of steam during their auditions. They start off strong and let their energy slowly dwindle. This is especially true during long speeches. You want to start off each beat with renewed energy.

7. Some actors overanalyze material and then forget to let it go when they do the actual audition. Analyzing material should just be a springboard for you to leap off when you

do the audition. Trust the work you've done in the waiting area and let yourself fly during the audition.

8. Don't use an empty chair as a prop. If there is a chair onstage and you've decided that sitting in it is not appropriate, get rid of it before you start. Don't put the chair between you and the auditors. Don't use it to pretend you're talking to an imaginary person. It'll always just look like an empty chair.

9. Sometimes you show up at an audition inappropriately dressed. You thought you were the blue-collar guy, and you find out you're the high-power executive. There's nothing you can do. Don't make a big deal about it. The less said the better. If they mention something, lightly say "I thought I was reading for the blue-collar guy role. Sorry." Just give yourself that extra ounce of imaginary belief and feel yourself in that expensive business suit.

Also, never enter making excuses, such as "Sorry, I'm late," "Just got the script right before I walked in," "Sorry, I have a cold today." The less said the better; just get on with your audition.

10. Actors sometimes make the mistake of being talking heads at an audition, forgetting to stay connected to their bodies. Be aware of how you're standing or sitting during an audition. Your body is part of your character. Your body is a great communication. It tells people all about you. Watch how people on the street hold themselves. You can see if a person is depressed, uptight, or in a good mood just by the way he holds himself. We're all communicating with our bodies all the time. Be aware of your posture. Don't slump when talking to the casting team; stand upright.

11. If you have trouble reading without glasses, by all means buy a pair for auditions. You might invest in a pair of rimless glasses just for reads. The less obtrusive the frame, the better.

12. Nothing infuriates a playwright or screenwriter more than seeing an actor change his carefully chosen words for words that the actor has decided to say. Quite often, the playwright or screenwriter will be at the audition room. Don't add *uh*'s or *um*'s to their script either. And never criticize the script.

13. If the audition read isn't going well, rather than asking to start over, remember that at any time you can change gears and make it go the way you want it. It's your audition; you're in charge. Never give up your creative power at an audition.

14. If you flub a line, fall down (literally), or drop the script, minimize the mistake with a little humor. Making fun of oneself is always a great equalizer in what might seem (to you) a disaster. It shows you're human.

15. Don't make too much of your part. If the part you're reading for is only a couple of lines, don't overact. Unless your line is something like "Rome is on fire!," keep the role in proper perspective. Figure out where your character (and lines) come into play in the script, and then see what happens after you exit. If you're playing a doorman who only says, "Will there be anything else, sir?," keep it simple. You're part of an ensemble of actors in the play or movie; just do your bit as honestly as you can.

16. Don't memorize all your lines at a cold-read audition. Even if it's a small role, you should refer to the script. Trying to remember what your next line is at an audition is a waste of energy. If you're auditioning for a commercial

and there is only one or two lines, then it's fine to learn them. In general, memorizing the first line of the text can be helpful in starting out the scene.

17. Actors sometimes play all the lines in the scene as if they had the same importance. There is no modulation. It's like listening to music at a very high volume. Generally, these actors haven't decided what the important moments in the scene are.

18. If you're auditioning on camera, try not to move around too much. Actors who move too much can move out of the frame. If the scene requires movement, keep it minimal and take your time. If you move too fast, you may go out of focus.

    When not talking, just listen. When other people are talking and your not directly involved, just listen. And be positive about doing nothing: just "be."

19. Don't avoid the fourth wall at your audition. The fourth wall is that imaginary wall that between you and the audition team. Actors, afraid of making eye contact with the audition team, sometimes do not look at the fourth wall when it is the most logical place to look. By using the fourth wall, the casting team can see more of you and the work you're doing.

20. Your part doesn't start with your first word. It really starts with your preparation and the moment before. When you find yourself trying to catch up at your audition, that usually indicates that you didn't prepare well. Before you say your first word, make sure you have a strong launchpad that will propel you into the first words of the first line.

21. Don't bring props to the audition room. You can pantomime whatever activity the script calls for. Props can

fall out of your hand or can bring unnecessary attention to insignificant actions.

22. Don't ask the casting director if you can read for another role. You're there to audition for the role you've been asked to audition for. If the casting director sees that you're right for another role, he'll suggest it. If he does, make sure to take your time reading the new role in the waiting area. You've obviously done something right so that they believe in you enough to give you another shot.

23. If something happens in the audition room that unfocuses you, say a telephone ringing or a door slamming, don't let it throw you. This happens quite often at auditions in an agent's office. Silently just acknowledge it to yourself and continue.

    If, in the agent's office, the agent asks you to please hold for a moment while he takes care of some business, stay concentrated, remain focused. Don't get annoyed at him; that won't help. This is his office, and business must be dealt with. When you're asked to continue, do so with grace and skill. Try to pick up exactly where you left off.

    Never be impolite or discourteous at any audition. Even if they're rude, take the high road. And don't allow their rudeness to affect your audition. Get more focused, not less. I realize that this can be difficult, but retaliating by being rude is a no-win for you.

24. Never apologize for your performance at an audition. Quite often, it's not as bad as you may imagine, and you might kill the possibility of a callback. Your perception of your work at an audition can be very different from the auditors. In general, apologizing for anything at the audition is a waste of time.

25. Beating yourself up after what you felt was a bad audition is pointless. This is not a paid performance, and they are very aware that you recently got the sides and were going on your hunches. What's of more value is try to see where you have gone off at the audition and make sure that it doesn't occur at the next one. There is always a next one, always.

I look for someone who is really all about the work, not about all the bullshit. I want to see someone who's focused on the work and has a real sense of himself. It's amazing how people sabotage themselves. They say things like, "I didn't have a chance to read the script." Or "What are you guys looking for?"

Risa Bramon Garcia, casting director

Chapter 5

50 THINGS YOU NEED TO KNOW ABOUT COLD READING FOR THEATER AUDITIONS

1. It all starts at home the day of the audition. You start to prepare for the audition when you get up. You want to make sure that you'll arrive at the audition positive and focused. Perhaps you could do some stretching or breathing. I personally like to go to the gym, have a nice workout, and get rid of any tension I may have.

2. Many people believe in visualizing, imagining how you want the audition to go. It's helpful to see yourself confident, open, and available. See yourself going in there and giving a slam-dunk audition.

3. Since this is a book on cold readings, we'll assume you don't have any sides for the play, but you may have been given some information about what they're looking for, such as what type of character you're auditioning for. You may want to dress accordingly. That doesn't mean go in an army uniform if it's the role of a soldier, just something

that might be appropriate and suggests soldier without going overboard.

I was at an audition where an actor was reading for the role of a bank robber and the actor brought a gun, a real gun, into the audition room—not a good idea.

4. Hopefully you'll have the luxury of not having to rush to get to the audition on time. You want to take your time, remain calm, and arrive at least twenty to thirty minutes early.

5. Smile. Be professional and friendly to whoever is running the auditions. You know the old adage: Today's secretary is tomorrow's casting director. You never know where people will end up.

6. When you get the sides, immediately find a seat and begin your work on the script. After the first read of the script, begin again and find the key words in the sentences. Figure out what you want to emphasize.

7. If the scene has a fair amount of small talk—such as "Nice day isn't it?"—you can bet there is something going on underneath. Generally, playwrights don't waste time with small talk unless it indicates something about the character and the scene. See if you can find out what your character is really saying, the subtext.

8. If a word is repeated in a scene, such as "you . . . you . . . you . . . ," don't say the word the same way each time. The emotion should progress from one "you" to the next. Perhaps you're realizing something about the other character. There can be a lot going on and a lot to express in just the repetition of a word.

9. Here's the bottom line on a cold read or any audition: Your job is to make us believe that you are the character

in the play or screenplay. Actors sometimes get caught up in the minutia and forget the big picture—what an audition is really all about. You must use everything in your power and creativity to make that character on the page come to life. Actors sometimes get upset about blowing a line or not getting a moment at the audition and then spend the rest of their audition sabotaging their work. If you believe, we'll believe; if you don't, we won't.

10. Find the important moments in the scene. Some actors play all the moments with the same emotion and intensity. Find which moments of the story are really important and be sure to land with those.

11. What is this scene about? What is the play about? If you don't have enough information from the sides to get a sense of what the play is about, then use your imagination.

12. Use variety in your performance at the audition. You can pick up the pace or slow it down to a crawl, especially for emphasis. Don't deliver all your lines exactly the same. Use pacing and emphasis to explicate the text and what is happening in the scene. Don't use emphasis just to call attention to you, the actor. We're only interested in the character and his story. Your job is to illuminate both.

13. Whatever you decide to do at your audition, keep it simple. Actors sometimes think that more is better at an audition; it's not. Sometimes the simplest gesture, the way you say a word, or a special look can do more than just yelling or crying.

14. Who is the character your playing? Once you get a take on him, figure out how you can identify with him. Two good questions to ask yourself after you read the script are: How am I like this character? How am I unlike this character? These questions may help you get inside the

piece quickly. However you can identify with the character will be helpful in your audition.

15. Where is the character? Where does the scene take place? A scene that takes place in a prison cell will play very differently than a scene at a party.

16. Does this scene take place in the present, the past, or the future?

17. What time of day or night does this scene take place? A scene that takes place at two in the afternoon will probably require a different energy than one that takes place at four in the morning.

18. What time of year is it? A scene that takes place in the dead of winter will play differently than one on a hot, humid summer day.

19. What is the character doing in this scene? Playing the actions in a scene are important, but remember, this is an audition. Don't overburden yourself with a lot of busy activities.

20. What does your character want (objective/intention), and what is preventing him from getting it (conflict)? Knowing and playing the intention and finding and playing the conflict is crucial to any scene.

21. Try to get a sense of what your character feels in this scene. Try to identify with the character's emotions; make the scene personal. Do his emotions change as the scene progresses? If so, how? Plot the arc of the emotional life in the scene.

22. What is the relationship between your character and the other character(s) in the scene? Do your feelings change toward the other character as the scene progresses? The description section sometimes offers clues as to the relationship of the characters.

23. Think about the your character's background, his history. Time permitting, you should think about the character's life before this scene takes place. What was his childhood like? His family?

24. Always note how far along in the play your scene is. The timing of the scene will indicate what changes your character has been through. If the scene is from early in the play—say, the first few pages—the relationships between the characters may not be fully developed. If the sides are from late in the play, you could assume that the characters are well developed. There is, of course, the chance that your character is meeting a new character in the play in a later scene.

25. After you've read the sides once or twice, go off somewhere where you can be alone and read the scenes out loud. You don't need to fully act out the scenes, just mark what you'd like to do at the audition.

   Be aware of the language that the playwright uses for your character. Saying the words out loud helps you feel comfortable with how your character speaks, the way he says his words. You may get an impulse on how your character speaks. Trust that impulse and let it develop until the moment they call you in to audition.

26. Don't work too hard at your audition. Sometimes actors go overboard at an audition. Their throat tightens and they muscularize their movements. In an attempt to make a emotional home run, they overdo—don't. Always stay relaxed and save some of that emotion for yourself. If it feels overly raw, it generally is too much. Pull back. You can pull back at any point during the audition.

27. When you are called in to the audition room, put on your professional mask. Assuming you've done your work on the scene and know what you want to do, enter the

audition room professionally. Enter as a professional, accessible, confident actor. You do not want to enter in character, especially if your character is extremely depressed or crazy. We put on our professional masks all the time. If you've ever had a job where you dealt with the public, you know you have to put on your professional mask before dealing with customers, even if you've had a terrible experience just before going to work.

Right beneath the surface is the work you've done on your character. When it's time to audition, you remove the professional mask and your character emerges.

28. Your entrance is a major part of any audition. The energy you bring into the room makes an important first impression. Let them know from that first entrance that you will be a joy to work with. I know that many actors feel insecure walking into the audition room. Some feel the casting people have all the power. This is not true. Remember they need you as much as you need them. They've got a play that they must get cast. They need actors. They need you!

29. Make eye contact with the people who are running the audition. Yes, they are watching you, judging you. Live with it. Try to make the best first impression that you can.

30. Don't shake everyone's hand on the auditioning team. They might be seeing fifty or more actors that day. At least one of those actors will have a cold or virus, which may get passed on to people on the team. No one wants a cold, so some casting directors will refuse to shake your hand—which makes for an awkward moment if you extend your hand.

But if they hold their hands out for you to shake, go right ahead. You may want to wash your hands after the audition so that you don't pick up anything. You're shaking hands with people who have been shaking hands with other people all day long. I know, it sounds a bit germ-phobic, but it may save you from getting a cold.

31. Be aware of your playing area. It's not necessary to walk right up to the casting team to say hello; you can do it from the playing area where you'll be working. Actors charging into the casting directors' space can seem intrusive.

32. If you have any questions about the scene or the character, by all means ask. But don't take up too much of their time discussing interpretation.

33. If they want to chat with you before the audition, you can take one of two actions:
    • You can choose to chat with them.
    • You can politely say, "I've done some preparation for this scene. Can we please talk after?" There is nothing wrong with this. If they know anything about actors and preparation, they will respect and value your request. I know many actors are intimidated by auditions and won't do this. But if you've emotionally prepared for a really tough scene, you need to let them know that your preparation might be in jeopardy. It's your call.

34. Make all your movements appropriate to the space your auditioning in. If you need to move about during the audition, adjust your movements to the space. A large theater requires a different amount of movement than a tiny rehearsal space.

35. The reader is generally not someone you can depend on to give you what you need in the scene at an audition. Hopefully, you've done your preparation outside in the waiting area. It's important that you listen to the words of the other character at the audition. Even if the reader doesn't

give you what you need, you can imagine what the scene is about and play it as you see it.

The same thing applies in a situation where you're auditioning with another actor and he's not giving you what you need. You must listen to what the character saying.

36. Don't get caught up in the rhythms of the reader if it doesn't support your preparation for the scene. Sometimes he reads too slowly or with little sense of urgency. Just do your work and don't be too concerned (or judgmental) of what the reader is doing.

37. Don't lock eyes with the reader. Actors have a tendency to lock eyes with the reader at an audition. It's unnatural and not very convincing. We don't do it in life; we shouldn't do it at an audition.

38. If the reader is reading lines for several different characters in the scene, you should react differently to each character. Your character's relationship is likely different for each of the other characters.

39. Keep all actions simple. If it's a romantic scene with passionate kissing, a gentle kiss on the cheek will do. When a scene calls for fighting, shoving, or violence, indicate the necessary movement in a simple, nonviolent way.

40. While reading at the audition, always control the pace. Don't be afraid to pause midsentence if it feels right to you. On the other hand, too many unnecessary pauses will become an ineffective device, so pause only when necessary. The more control you have over the material you're reading, the more you will impress the casting team.

41. No need to be overly thankful to the reader at the end of the audition, even if he gave you something to play off. A pleasant, professional thank you is all you need.

42. At the end of the audition, look at the casting team and simply say thank you. If they want to talk to you or want you to read another scene, they'll let you know.

43. At the end of your audition, don't signal through your facial expressions that you thought your audition was lousy. Maintain neutrality. You may have thought you sucked, but they may have seen what they needed.

44. If they want to talk with you after your audition, try to be open, positive, confident, and calm. Quite often the reason they want to chat with you is to find out if you're someone they would like to have in their production. They probably liked your audition and now want to make sure that you're a team player.

45. While talking with auditors after your audition, never put down anyone that you've worked with before. Always find something positive to say about past directors, playwrights, and actors you've worked with.

46. Leave all auditions confident, upbeat, and professional. Go away smiling.

47. It's always a good idea to write down the names of the people who were at your audition for future reference.

48. Sending a thank-you note to the casting director who was at the audition is always a nice gesture. Let go of the audition and go on with your life. Let it go!

49. ANSWERING THE "SO WHAT HAVE YOU BEEN UP TO LATELY?" QUESTION

Throughout your acting career you will constantly be asked at interviews and auditions "So what have you been up to lately?" It's very important that you know how you want to respond—in advance. Interested casting directors, agents, and directors ask this question of actors to get some sense of them.

Your answer to this question should be prepared well in advance. Your response shouldn't be more than a minute or a minute and a half. It should include all recent significant activity in the business. It should not include too much about your personal life—perhaps where you grew up, what school you went to. Your answer should be positive, upbeat, and confident. It should not be memorized even though all the information should be. Your answer should be spontaneous and positive.

This is not the time to put down that director that you hated working with in your last play. The belief is if you're putting down that last director to these new people, you might very well badmouth these folks at your next interview. Not a negative word should be spoken while answering this question. Everyone wants to work with a winner, and your answer should imply confidence and professionalism.

Don't lie! There is nothing worse than being caught in a lie of any size during an interview or audition. It invalidates you as a potential candidate. Trust me, it's not worth it.

50. THE LEGITIMATE TALENT AGENT AUDITION

I felt it's important to deal with the legitimate talent agent audition. These auditions generally take place in the agent's office. The legit agent sends you out on theater (or film or TV) auditions. Generally, they'll ask if you have a reel or to prepare a couple of contrasting monologues for your interview. On occasion, they may have some cold-read material that they'll ask you to read.

If you're auditioning for a legit agent in his office, here are some things that are going through his mind during your audition:

- Will I be able to get this actor work?
- Do I get calls for his type?

- I wonder what his range is?

- What types of roles would he be right for?

- How would he do in film, television, or on daytime serials?

- Does he have enough training, or should I suggest some coaches or schools to him?

- Will I feel comfortable working with him, or will he be a problem?

- Will he be reliable, show up at auditions, and be professional?

- How serious is he about his career?

- Is he shopping around with many other agents?

- Is everything on his résumé truthful?

- Is there anything in his past that I should know about?

Here are some questions that may be asked of you in the agent's office after your audition. Again, before going to his office, write out your responses and be prepared to spontaneously answer these questions at the interview.

- Why are you interested in show business?

- What does your career mean to you?

- Why would this agency be right for you and your needs as an actor?

- What are your career goals?

- Do you plan on living just in New York or are you thinking of being bicoastal?

- Where do you primarily want to focus: film, theater or television?

- Besides your career, what other things do you do?

- Have you worked with other agents before? Have you ever been signed before?

- What kind of things have you been doing on your own for your career?

- Where do you see yourself in five (ten) years?

- Why do you want to be an actor?

Think about your responses to all of these questions. Write them out. Don't memorize your answers but be ready to call upon the information in an impromptu manner.

It always helps to understand what you're auditioning for. Ask yourself, "What is this play about? Who is the character?" Actors come in and they have the sides, and they are not given any direction. It's the actor's interpretation of what this character should be.

Jerry Beaver, casting director

Chapter 6

ANALYSIS OF
COLD READING PLAYS

What follows are scenes from two plays, *The Danger of Strangers* and *Hardball*. Read through the scenes, and then read the breakdown analysis that follows each of them. Next, find a scene partner and do a cold-read audition of the scenes as if you both were auditioning for the roles. It will be useful to review all the basic cold-reading skills given in the first two chapters.

THE DANGER OF STRANGERS

By Glenn Alterman

The living room of a one-bedroom apartment in the West 50s overlooking 9th Avenue in New York City. Bright sunlight is shining in from a window. An attractive man and a woman are sitting opposite each other, just finishing their coffee. A small coffee table separates them. His sport jacket is neatly folded on the back of his chair. His tie his loosened and the top couple of buttons of his shirt are open. He's sweating but trying not to show it. She, on the other hand, doesn't seem to notice the heat at all. In her light beige blouse and tan skirt, she seems cool and crisp. There is a polite, yet playful sexual tension in the air. A small, rotating floor fan attempts to cool them off.

SHE: More?

HE: Hm?

SHE: More coffee?

HE: No, thanks.

SHE: Sure?

HE: Yeah?

SHE: You sure?

HE: Uh-huh. *(A wink in his voice.)* But I am tempted.

SHE: Are you?

HE: You are tempting me.

SHE: *(Slightly coy.)* Am I?

HE: *(Leaning in a bit.)* C'mon, you know you are.
        (SHE looks down at her coffee cup, lifts it to her lips, takes a sip. He watches her, then smiles.)

SHE: What's so funny?

HE: Funny?

SHE: You're smiling.

HE: *(Playing with her.)* Am I?

SHE: C'mon, you know you are.

HE: I don't know, just seems funny.

SHE: What?

HE: My bein' here.

SHE: Does it?

HE: See, you really don't know me.

SHE: No, I don't.

HE: So you don't know that this isn't me. Well it's me, yeah, sure. But it's not like typical me.

SHE: No?

HE: No, I don't usually do this.

SHE: Do what?

HE: This: come up to a strange woman's apartment, middle of the afternoon, on my lunch hour.

SHE: No?

HE: No, s'a first.

SHE: Hm.

HE: See, I'm basically an old-fashioned guy.

SHE: Yeah?

HE: Big believer in the old "how do you do's." Y'know like introductions, formalities, like that. Even at work, everything's always in order; my desk, perfect, every pencil . . .

SHE: How do you do?

HE: Hm?

SHE: *(Smiling, slowly, each word deliberate.)* How . . . do . . . you . . . do?

HE: No, I'm serious here.

SHE: So am I. It's Herb, right?

HE: Yeah, Herb, Herbie.

SHE: *(Offering her hand.)* How do you do, Herbie?

HE: *(Shaking her hand, slightly confused.)* I'm fine, . . . thanks.

SHE: Good. See how simple that was? Now we know each other.

HE: Well . . .

SHE: So how about a drink?

HE: Drink?

SHE: Scotch all right?

HE: No, thanks. Told ya, I gotta get back.

SHE: C'mon, surely you've got time for a small cocktail.

HE: I can't, I'm sorry.

SHE: *(Softly seductive.)* Have a drink with me, Herb. C'mon, nice, cool scotch on the rocks. Lemon twist. Cool you right off. You're sweating, you know that?

HE: S'hot, yeah.

SHE: Yeah it is. Must be what, at least ninety today.

HE: At least.

SHE: So how about that scotch?

HE: *(Half smiling.)* You don't give up, do ya?

SHE: *(Getting up.)* On the rocks? *(HE just looks at her.)* Or do you like it straight up?

HE: *(A slight pause, then smiling.)* Couple of cubes . . . not much scotch . . . little water. Short one.

SHE: Coming right up. *(SHE goes over to the counter, he watches her. SHE takes a couple of glasses from the cupboard, starts to make their drinks. SHE notices him watching her, smiles.)*

HE: *(Smiling.)* Short one.

SHE: I know, I heard you.

   (SHE starts cutting lemon peels for their drinks. HE turns back around, opens a couple of buttons on his shirt, takes his tie off, rolls up his sleeves, looks around. The lights come down on everything except for her. HE freezes

in place. She speaks straight out, seems more timid, upset. Her alibi:)

I had a few drinks; all right maybe more than a few. I don't know. I've been . . . My sister died here recently. She was murdered, in the bedroom. They still don't know . . . We were close, Claire and I.

I'd been straightening out some of her things, putting them into boxes. I decided to take a nap. Went into the bedroom to lie down. I was almost asleep, but I heard something. Felt like someone was in the room. It was dark. I looked up and he was standing there, this man. Just . . . Maybe I'd left the door open, I don't know. But he was standing there in the dark. I could barely see him, but I saw the knife, the kitchen knife! He told me if I screamed, made a sound, he'd kill me. He told me to get undressed. I was numb, didn't know what to do. I couldn't move! He started unbuttoning my blouse. I just . . . I let him, said, "Please, don't, don't!" He got on top of me. I felt . . . I heard . . . his zipper. His face, right in mine. His eyes, breath! Then . . . It was like the room started spinning! I just went crazy, I guess, threw him off me! All my strength! The knife fell. The two of us scrambling in the dark. I grabbed it—the knife! He was right there. He was . . . I . . . *(SHE jabs in the air.)* IN! IN! I kept . . . *(Jabbing the air.)* IN! IN! Then he . . . he fell, fell down. I . . . He tried . . . ! He would have raped me, you understand?! I had no . . . ! He's probably the one who killed Claire. Don't you see? He . . . he tried. He . . . He . . .

(The lights quickly come back up, the scene continues.)

HE: S'a nice place ya got here.

SHE: Thanks, s'my sister's.

ANALYSIS OF THE DANGER OF STRANGERS

First off, you must decide on the given circumstances in the scene. What is this scene about? Two strangers meet, and it appears that a scene of seduction is taking place. You need to determine how your character feels about the person he or she is talking with and why he or she is there.

WHO ARE THE CHARACTERS AND WHAT DO THEY WANT?

After your first read of the material you'll get a first impression, a gut reaction to your character. Trust what you feel. Ask yourself, "How am I like him? How am I not like him?" Personalize, identify, and make him you, and you him.

You'll need to determine what his objective is. What does he want? Why is he there in the first place? What does she want? It's her apartment: Why did she invite him up? Is it sex or perhaps something more? The monologue at the end of the scene gives you some insight into the woman you're playing. Make solid choices about how the monologue connects to the previous events.

One clue in playing thrillers: Don't play the end of the scene—her monologue at the end of the scene—at the beginning. The monologue is supposed to surprise the audience. If you play the information that you learn in the monologue at the beginning of the scene, the surprise will be minimal. The playwright wants to surprise the audience when the monologue comes.

WHAT IS THE RELATIONSHIP BETWEEN YOUR CHARACTER AND THE OTHER CHARACTER(S)?

You must always determine what the relationship is between your character and the person you're talking to. What does he/she feel about the person he/she is talking to? They are strangers who are getting to know each other. You want to establish what their relationship is at this time in the play. Since they've just met, there isn't much history between these two characters. At this point in the play, things seem cordial with a sexual undercurrent. There is an attraction, a playfulness.

WHERE IS THE CHARACTER?

The location in this scene is an important feature. We learn that it takes place in "The living room of a one-bedroom apartment in the West 50s overlooking 9th Avenue in New York City. Bright sunlight is shining in from a window. A small coffee table separates them."

The play takes place in the living room of the woman's apartment on a hot summer day. The way the heat affects them might be an important clue to who these two people are and what they might want.

WHAT IS THE CHARACTER DOING?

Depending on which character you're playing, decide what actions he or she makes in this scene. The two are having coffee. How you hold the cup, drink the coffee, look at each other, smile, move around in your chair—all indicate something about your character's interest in the other person and how he or she feels (or appear to feels).

WHAT DOES HE WANT?

At every cold-read audition, you must make a decision about what your character wants. Based on your intention, your character's behavior and actions should demonstrate what your character wants.

He, it seems, is there to have sex with this attractive, albeit, mysterious woman. The actor playing the man must create behavior and personalize this desire. How cool he is under the circumstances is affected by the heat in her apartment.

Her intention is more mysterious. We just know she wants him to stay there with her. It is up to the actor to find her reason for wanting him to stay. Perhaps it's sex. Perhaps she's lonely. Her final monologue might give you some of the clues you're looking for. No matter what you decide, go with it fully at the audition. If, after the read, the director gives you an adjustment, you must be willing to shift gears and go with his suggestion. Especially in thrillers such as this play, the creative staff, who are familiar with the whole play, probably know more than you.

CHARACTER CHOICES IN THE THRILLER

The Danger of Strangers is a thriller. When you're given the sides for a play and are told (or you realize) that it's a thriller, make sure that your choices about the character are consistent with the genre. You realize just by this scene that there are surprises in this play. You can assume if it's a thriller that there will be more surprises as the play goes along. All you can do is play the events as they unfold in the play, moment to moment. This scene happens to be at the beginning of the play, and you can be certain there is more to discover about both characters. But for now, stay in the moment of what's happening.

THE TITLE OF THE PLAY

The title, *The Danger of Strangers*, gives us a clue as to what type of play it might be. The character names, He and She, indicate something about the story being told.

We realize by the cat-and-mouse quality to the scene that games are being played between these two strangers. We realize that they really don't know each other and yet are having a cup of coffee in the woman's apartment. There is a coy, playful, yet dangerous undertone to the scene. You need to decide how much you want to reveal about your character as the scene progresses. In this scene, the woman seems to be more aggressive, more seductive. The man may be a victim or a playful participant. Whatever you decide about him, proceed, as always, with full conviction.

BODY LANGUAGE AND EYE CONTACT

In this scene, the two characters spend some time sitting in their chairs talking and studying each other. There is a lot an actor can do with just a slight shift of his body in a chair, or a specific movement that indicates something about the character the actor is playing. A look, stare, or gaze at the other character at a pivotal moment might also tell us about the character they're playing. In the cold-read audition, there isn't much time to plan what, when, or where you'll make your move.

How she moves, the way she holds her body will tell us a great deal about the way she is trying to seduce him. How he sits, his body language, will tell us how aware or unaware his character might be

THE SWITCH IN THE SCENE

Her monologue at the end of the scene reveals a great deal about the woman. We get an entirely different perspective about her. The beginning of the scene is a setup and then a sudden switch. What's real and what is not real about her is a choice you must make and go with at your audition. Who she is, her truth, cannot be determined by just this one scene. So you must make a decision based on what you know now and go with it.

The beauty of switches in scenes, what makes them most effective, is that we (the audience) don't see them coming. But when they do—bam! As in all good acting, take each moment at the audition as it comes, playing it as honestly as you can.

HARDBALL

By Michael Bettencourt, Robert E. Ozasky, and Dean B. Kaner

The protagonist of Hardball *is Dean Kaner's grandfather, Henry Kaner. In his early twenties, Henry Kaner had been a pitching phenom for a semipro baseball team in Superior, Wisconsin. Everyone expected him to move up to the majors, and in fact he was offered a contract by the St. Louis Browns. What made his story dramaworthy in Dean's eyes was the fact that Henry was the son of Orthodox Jewish parents who had emigrated from Lithuania to escape the pogroms and because of their efforts to create a better life, Henry Kaner, twenty-two, had been offered the chance to reach the American dream through that most American game, baseball.*

The catch, of course, was that he would have had to play on Saturdays. In the end, he said thanks, but no thanks, choosing religion and family (his father was in the beginning stages of Alzheimer's, which in 1922 was a new condition, only named in 1906) over what probably would have been a lucrative career.

This scene takes place at the end of the Sabbath and sets the stage for the decision that Henry will have to make.

ACT 1, SCENE 3

Saturday night. Kaner porch. HENRY looks skyward. MORRIE next to him.

MORRIE: Come on!
HENRY: Wait.

MORRIE: For what?

HENRY: Wait.

MORRIE: For what?!

HENRY: I have to wait until it comes.

MORRIE: Ya got two stars already—there and there.

HENRY: It's got to be three.

MORRIE: You don't even really believe in this stuff.

HENRY: I believe in it enough.

MORRIE: There's gonna be three anyway, there always is, so just get a jump on the third and let's get going.

HENRY: Just wait.
> (They wait. The star comes.)

HENRY: Done.

MORRIE: So let's hoof it.

HENRY: Wait! *Barukh atah Adonai Elohaynu melekh ha-olam—*

MORRIE: Oh, man—

HENRY: *—ha-mavdil bayn kodesh l'chol*—Done.

MORRIE: You didn't finish it.

HENRY: I did enough.

MORRIE: Even I know that's not enough.

HENRY: It's enough.

MORRIE: Half-in, half-not. Wait for the stars but don't mouth out the prayer. A little Jewish and a lot Jewish—why are you walking this line? It's gonna ruin things for you.

HENRY: Things are fine.

MORRIE: Like today? We lost because of you—well, because of not you—your arm, your curve, your slider—not there, pal, just not there because your arm had to be all Shabbos all day. Farnsworthy was sniffing around again.

HENRY: Yeah?

MORRIE: Yeah.

HENRY: And.

MORRIE: Asked Coach some more about you.

HENRY: About me.

MORRIE: Yeah.

HENRY: What'd Coach say?

MORRIE: What'd'ya think he said?

HENRY: What did he say?

MORRIE: "Hanks's a good boy—arm like a bullwhip. Comes from a good home—Jewish, but good." Coach thinks he's being big-hearted when he says stuff like that—

HENRY: Coach is all right.

MORRIE: Coach is not all right when it comes to the twelve tribes.

HENRY: And why do you care? I don't hear you calling yourself a Jew much, so why'd you care if someone calls a Jew a name?

MORRIE: Doesn't mean I can take kike, hymie, yid, and hebe like I'm taking an aspirin!

HENRY: You play baseball on Shabbos.

MORRIE: And you know what about that? Farnsworthy talked to me, too. Again.

HENRY: Make you an offer?

MORRIE: Not yet. Maybe he will, maybe not—be nice to go down to St. Louis and try to get in. But not my point. He talked to me because he saw me play. Saturday or not,

Shabbos or not, he saw me play. I find that I play on Saturday, lightning doesn't strike me dead. God doesn't turn my third base into a burning bush. I take in a movie on Friday night and the world doesn't spin off its axle. Farnsworthy likes you—Coach seems to think he'd like to give you a ten-day offer.

HENRY: Maybe the big league'd stop games Friday, Saturday for me.

MORRIE: Yeah—and my foreskin'll grow back by the next full moon.

HENRY: Wouldn't do you any good anyway.

MORRIE: Look, Hank, it's a business with these guys.

HENRY: Business—

MORRIE: These guys don't care Shabbos, Yom Kippur—it's all about the money.

HENRY: Shouldn't all be about the money.

MORRIE: It's about the money, simple and pure, Hank, that's American life for you—your folks know that—that's why they came.

HENRY: Mama, maybe—a long maybe—not Papa.

MORRIE: You're as bad your old man, he thinks the game is the blueprint of life, clipping away and talking about the Sefirot and the Kabbalah—lucky the guy in the chair's got any hair left! And that guy's sometimes me!

HENRY: Papa never started out to be a barber.

MORRIE: Well, it's too bad that that's where he got ended up, but it's where he ended up—and you got a chance to get ended up someplace very different, Henry.

HENRY: If I play Saturday.

MORRIE: Plain as the swerve on your curve.

HENRY: *(Laughing.)* Man—

MORRIE: Look at us, Hank, sitting under the three stars. Your family's got about as many nickels to rub together as mine. Your papa cuts hair, you work the fire station nights, your mama takes in some piecework, and David—he'll be the required doctor in the family. I got the same routine—my pop working the factory, my mom typing letters in an office, brother and sister listening to jazz and saying "beeswax" to tick off my parents. Wouldn't it be nice if Farnsworthy offered both of us a trip downtown, huh? Huh?

HENRY: Yes.

MORRIE: Those nickels'd turn into dollars and we could tuck 'em in our parents' pockets and never worry about them having to worry about anything. Not a bad thing for the son to do for the family, eh?

HENRY: Not bad at all.

MORRIE: And you'd let a Saturday get in the way of doing that kind of goodness for the ones that raised you—what's that look?

HENRY: It would be great, wouldn't it?

MORRIE: What's that?

HENRY: To get a trip downtown.

MORRIE: I didn't hear you.

HENRY: I said—

MORRIE: It would, wouldn't it? Look at your face!

HENRY: Everything is so—clean—when I'm out there, Morrie. So clear. Me, the batter—that's it. All—together—

MORRIE: Would you kill to play? Would you kill to play?

HENRY: Do you mean would it kill me not to play?

MORRIE: Exactly.

(HENRY doesn't answer.)

MORRIE: Your whole face gives me the answer. You'll have to give it up if you stay around here—your fate will get you— *(In a "monster" voice.)* —the weight of the mother will crush you—

(HENRY and MORRIE growl, monsterlike. They laugh. MORRIE points to the sky.)

MORRIE: We got even more stars out. Satisfied? If we hurry, we can get there before the second feature starts.

(They start to exit.)

MORRIE: Want to hear an ancient Chinese proverb about baseball? "Man with four balls cannot walk."

HENRY: What's that go to do with anything?

MORRIE: Got nothing to do with anything except to make you laugh.

HENRY: It makes me laugh.

(And off they go, MORRIE waddling as if he's got four balls. Lights. Transition.)

ANALYSIS OF HARDBALL

Before your cold-reading audition of this scene you must first determine all the given circumstances of the scene. Here's a quick checklist.

- What is this scene about? The scene gives you an indication of what the play is about. The title, *Hardball*, also provides clues.

- Who is the character? Each character is clearly drawn. Your job is to understand the character, identify with him, and by making specific choices bring him to life at the audition.

- What is the relationship between your character and the other character in the scene? The playwright has created a relationship of two caring friends. Your job is to find a way to empathize with both viewpoints and make their discussion about baseball meaningful and urgent.

- Where are the characters in this scene? You're told right up front about the time and place. Imagine what life was like in Michigan in 1922. The scene starts out on the porch.

- What is your character doing? See if you can find actions that will bring your character to life. By reading what the text tells you about them and seeing what they have to say to each other you should be able to come up with some valid actions.

- What is your character feeling at the start of the scene? Does his feelings change as the scene progresses? What effect does the discussion have on his emotions during the scene? Do his emotions change as the characters present their arguments?

- What does he want? Each character is very clear about what he wants. Baseball is the dream, the challenge.

- What is preventing him (the obstacle) from getting what he wants? Certainly religion is the main obstacle. Neither of these men is wealthy. Their families work hard to get ahead. A baseball career, aside from the fame, would give them money to help their families.

- What's at stake? See if you can discover what's at stake for each of these characters. Once you find what's at stake, you must play the scene with urgency. All auditions must have some urgency, what's at stake, to make the characters alive.

- How are you similar to your character? How are you different from your character? Find a way to identify with the character you are playing by personalizing. Remember, all characters that you play are you. The more you can bring your own sense of urgency to the scene, the better your audition will be.

Here are some things to keep in mind when auditioning with this scene.

- First, we learn that we're on the Kener porch in Superior, Michigan, and the year is 1922. The place and date should affect some of the acting choices that you'll make at the audition. Life was certainly different in 1922 than it is now.
- The scene (and conflict) deals with a career in baseball versus religious beliefs. Both characters have a point of view (and intention) on this subject, and in your audition you must find a way to personalize your character's position.
- The relationship between these two men is key to playing this scene. There is a closeness, a concern for each other, that should come into play. Notice the humor in the scene, the way they kid each other.
- There is urgency in their conversation that comes out of just how much baseball means to them. You can see what's at stake by the way they talk about the game.
- If they could make it in baseball, they could help their families out financially. This concern for family tells you something about their characters.

Chapter 7

EXERCISES FOR
COLD READING PLAYS

W hat follows are some practice audition scenes. Don't forget to review all the previous information on cold readings for scenes. What I suggest is that you and another actor use the following scenes as exercises in cold readings. Allow yourselves fifteen to twenty minutes to read the material, and then do them as if they were a real audition. After your auditions, evaluate how you felt you've done. Next, try another scene. Again, allow yourself twenty minutes or so to do your work, and then treat it as an audition. The more things you can incorporate from the checklists the better. Obviously, you won't be able to do *all* the things on the lists, but certainly always incorporate given circumstances and personalizing in all your exercise work.

I'M BREATHING THE WATER NOW

By Bashore Halow

ACT I

In the center of the stage, suspended from the ceiling, there is a large limb from which hangs a nooselike foot swing. Stage right there is a Lay-Z-Boy recliner in which GRANDMA is seated, perhaps for the whole play. There can be some clutter about her. At the play's open, lights rise to suggest the interior of a dense, richly green forest. Standing in front of the foot swing is JEFFREY AS NARRATOR. His eyes are closed, and his head lolls about dreamily.

JEFFREY AS NARRATOR: Hear that? Mosquitoes. A big buzz of them. High hummin'. Mosquitoes. It's 'cause of the swamp. Neck of Land is full of them. Walk half a mile in any direction and eventually you'll need wading boots. We got Po Creek to the west and the James River wraps around from the north down along the east side here.

    The south is just plain old mud, we don't have a name for that, just the road that runs through it which everyone around here calls Cus Road. There are so many potholes people drive over it going "goddamn son of a bitch."

    All this water makes for some fertile soil though, and we got farms around here like you never did see. Anything'll grow. On our property, we grow corn and soybeans and two big fields of alfalfa because we make hay for the horses. Tennessee walkers. My mother loves them. Rides the fence lines with her gelding. Private. *(Laughs.)* Makes sure that her borders are all secure.

    (Lights change to suggest the interior of the main house and the room in which GRANDMA is seated. She is in hysterics.)

GRANDMA: Jeffrey!

JEFFREY AS NARRATOR: My grandmother.

GRANDMA: Jeffrey! Oh dear! Where are you off to, darlin'? Are you in a hurry? Come here and sit with me for just a moment, please. I'm so blue. I'm so lonely. *(She begins to cry.)*

JEFFREY: What are you upset about?

GRANDMA: Everything! Everything, I tell you. Coo is so mean to me!

JEFFREY: What has mama done now?

GRANDMA: Hold my hand, darlin'.

JEFFREY: Don't be upset.

GRANDMA: Hold my hand.

JEFFREY: I am holding your hand.

GRANDMA: She is so mean.

JEFFREY: Yes, I know.

GRANDMA: She came in here and said the most awful things to me.

JEFFREY: What did she say?

GRANDMA: And yelled at me.

JEFFREY: I'm sorry.

GRANDMA: Have you eaten your lunch yet?

JEFFREY: No, ma'am.

GRANDMA: I haven't eaten my lunch either. They don't feed me.

JEFFREY: I'll get you something. What do you want?

GRANDMA: No one feeds me.

JEFFREY: I'll ask Rosina.

GRANDMA: Coo got mad at me because I wouldn't eat my lunch.

JEFFREY: Were you hungry?

GRANDMA: It was perfectly awful. Rosina made the most

terrible lunch in the world. She is a terrible maid and a worse cook. She made all sorts of terrible things and she wanted me to eat them and I refused.

JEFFREY: She made chicken.

GRANDMA: And now I am being persecuted. Oh God! Why is this happening to me? I wish I would die!

JEFFREY: Now, Grandma.

GRANDMA: Your mother told Rosina not to make me anything to eat. Not even a little pan of cornbread. Nothin'.

JEFFREY: I'll talk to her.

GRANDMA: Will you? Try to make her understand.

JEFFREY: I will.

GRANDMA: She won't listen to you. You two are too much alike.

JEFFREY: What?

GRANDMA: It's true. That's why you're always fighting.

JEFFREY: Well, it won't hurt to try.

GRANDMA: Oh, thank you, Jeffrey. You're a comfort to an old woman.

JEFFREY: *(Dismissingly.)* Ohhh.

GRANDMA: Do you want a piece of candy? I have a piece of candy over here. *(It takes her forever to find a piece of candy. Appropriate mumbling.)* I have to eat candy because they don't feed me. Look over there on my nightstand, darlin', and see if you can find a piece of candy. There should be a small bag of nonpareils or . . .

JEFFREY: M and Ms?

GRANDMA: What?

JEFFREY: These? M and M's?

GRANDMA: Oh! Let me see. Yes, these. Do you want an M and M?

JEFFREY: No, thank you.

GRANDMA: I have to live on chocolate. Do you want to watch something on the TV?

JEFFREY: No, but if you do, I'll turn it on.

GRANDMA: I don't care. I'm so bored. Don't ever get old, Jeffrey. Nobody should ever grow as old as me.

JEFFREY: Everyone in the whole town admires you.

GRANDMA: What?

JEFFREY: I said, everyone in the whole town admires you.

GRANDMA: Lotta trash. I don't have any friends. All my friends are dead. Do you want another M and M?

JEFFREY: OK. Give me one. I'll eat it.

GRANDMA: Don't eat too many. They're all I've got to live on.

JEFFREY: If you want. I'll go into the kitchen and fix you a plate of something myself. Rosina has a plate of chicken in the fridge. Would you like that?

GRANDMA: Whenever I used to be able to walk. I used to go into the kitchen and make my own cornbread. I used to make a small little pan of cornbread in the afternoon and that's all that I would eat the whole day, except at night, and then I would maybe open up a can of something and put it on a plate . . . oh, it didn't matter much what it was. I would just fend for myself thataway.

JEFFREY: Well, can I make you something?

GRANDMA: It's terrible to be so old. Do you know how old I am?

JEFFREY: Yes.

GRANDMA: I'm ninety-seven years old.

JEFFREY: You're going to live to be a hundred.

GRANDMA: That would be just awful. Sit down here next to me.

JEFFREY: I can't, Grandma. I have to go to rehearsal.

GRANDMA: Are you doing another play over at the college?

JEFFREY: Yes, Grandma.

GRANDMA: Now what's the name of this one?

JEFFREY: *La Cage Aux Folles.*

GRANDMA: Oh my! I never heard of that one. I hope you got a real pretty girl to play opposite you.

JEFFREY: Well . . .

GRANDMA: Your granddaddy would be proud of you. You are the third in the family to go the college. Your mother went. She rode her horse to graduation. She was crazy.

JEFFREY: Well, I have to go.

GRANDMA: She road her horse to graduation and ran that poor John Moody into Po Creek.

JEFFREY: Grandma . . .

GRANDMA: We all laughed about that, I'll tell you. But she didn't have to do that. He was just sweet on her is all.

JEFFREY: Grandma, I have to go.

GRANDMA: Oh . . . yes. You're going to be late.

JEFFREY: Is that OK? I'll be back after rehearsal and I'll sit with you.

GRANDMA: Oh, Jeffrey, before you go, will you tell me something?

JEFFREY: What's that, Grandma?

GRANDMA: What's the best way to kill yourself?

JEFFREY: Oh, Grandma, come on. I'll sit with you some more later. Or when I have to do my homework tonight, I'll bring it down here and read with you. OK?

GRANDMA: I used to know a woman in town. She was a very good friend of mine. The best. What was her name?

JEFFREY: Prunella Williams.

GRANDMA: Yes. Have I told you this story before?

JEFFREY: Yes.

GRANDMA: Oh . . .

(He starts to go.)

GRANDMA: She went to the Colonial House and had herself a big steak dinner, then she rented herself a room there and went to sleep with a bag tied around her head. Do you think that would be a nice way to kill yourself?

JEFFREY: No. It sounds awful.

GRANDMA: The next morning they found her. She was asleep. She died in her sleep.

JEFFREY: She choked to death! She wasn't asleep, she was dead!

GRANDMA: She didn't have to pay for her room. The Colonial House picked up the check.

JEFFREY: Well, that was nice. Look, I gotta go.

GRANDMA: *(Lamenting.)* Oooooh. Good-bye, darlin'. Thank you for sitting with an old woman.

JEFFREY: Oh, I don't mind.

GRANDMA: *(Insurance that he'll return.)* I love you.

JEFFREY: I love you too, Grandma.

THE DEAD BOY

By Joe Pintauro

SCENE 12

The YOUNG PRIEST is now aware that FATHER DAVIS is his future self.

FATHER DAVIS: I know where you came from.

YOUNG PRIEST: We have different memories.

FATHER DAVIS: Just another bad kid who thought God's grace would reinvent him.

YOUNG PRIEST: We're different.

FATHER DAVIS: Who now walks around like a self-appointed little saint.

YOUNG PRIEST: You lost faith. Not me.
(FATHER DAVIS holds him by the wrist. The YOUNG PRIEST slips away.)

FATHER DAVIS: Come here.

YOUNG PRIEST: Don't try anything.

FATHER DAVIS: I can help you. Just let me . . . *(FATHER DAVIS catches him by the arm.)*

YOUNG PRIEST: What are you trying . . . ?

FATHER DAVIS: Come sit.

YOUNG PRIEST: Let me go. I don't want you. I want God. The Blessed Mother. I want . . .

FATHER DAVIS: I'm the only one who can help you.
(The YOUNG PRIEST gets free.)

YOUNG PRIEST: No. I'll die a good priest.

FATHER DAVIS: How can you die a good priest?

YOUNG PRIEST: YOU'RE NOT DEAD YET.

FATHER DAVIS: Ha ha ha . . .

YOUNG PRIEST: You have time.

FATHER DAVIS: Very cute.

YOUNG PRIEST: I can save the both of us. Give me your hand. *(The YOUNG PRIEST grabs FATHER DAVIS's hand and places it on the YOUNG PRIEST's chest.)* Feel this heart . . .

FATHER DAVIS: *(Overlap.)* It's dead.

YOUNG PRIEST: Every beat is for the love of God.
(FATHER DAVIS grabs the YOUNG PRIEST's hand and places it on FATHER DAVIS's chest.)

FATHER DAVIS: Now you feel this heart, ice cold.

YOUNG PRIEST: Pray with me?

FATHER DAVIS: *(He sings.)* Silent Dad, Silent house. Gun on the table . . .

YOUNG PRIEST: I don't know what you're . . .

FATHER DAVIS: Mister Fox?

YOUNG PRIEST: Never heard of him.

FATHER DAVIS: Mother has a migraine. Dad's in the cellar all day and night.

YOUNG PRIEST: That's not me.

FATHER DAVIS: Oil truck's pumping oil into Mr. Fox's house next door. November. Older boys play cards around his table . . .

YOUNG PRIEST: Don't remember.

FATHER DAVIS: . . . but the old Fox is not there, is he? You see one boy at a time going upstairs, passing the window on the landing. One comes down, the other goes up. Where do they go after the landing?

YOUNG PRIEST: I don't want to . . .

FATHER DAVIS: To the attic to look at his pornography.

YOUNG PRIEST: Gettin' outta here.

> *(YOUNG PRIEST runs. FATHER DAVIS catches him and wrestles with him. The YOUNG PRIEST fights back but is being overcome.)*

FATHER DAVIS: You ring his bell. You're only thirteen . . .

YOUNG PRIEST: Not listening.

FATHER DAVIS: . . . to stand naked before a man your father's age who kneels before you . . .

YOUNG PRIEST: *(Overlap.)* DON'T SAY IT!

FATHER DAVIS: You look down at him through clouds, your head's as high as the sun. Now the boy is a king.

YOUNG PRIEST: I'm not listening.

FATHER DAVIS: You ring his bell the next day, and the next day and day after day . . .

> *(FATHER DAVIS has the YOUNG PRIEST in his grasp.)*

YOUNG PRIEST: I DID PENANCE.

FATHER DAVIS: You imagined God.

YOUNG PRIEST: We have given hope to the people.

FATHER DAVIS: Your faith will end.

YOUNG PRIEST: Let me end with it.

FATHER DAVIS: You'll become me. Yes.

> *(The YOUNG PRIEST starts to sob. FATHER DAVIS picks him up from behind and throws him down straddling the bench behind him like two men on a horse.)*

YOUNG PRIEST: Don't hurt me.

FATHER DAVIS: Gonna help you.

YOUNG PRIEST: What do you want to . . . ?

FATHER DAVIS: I want you to . . .

YOUNG PRIEST: *(Overlap.)* Don't touch me.

FATHER DAVIS: . . . go to another city. Get a job.

YOUNG PRIEST: *(Overlap.)* What're you trying to . . . ?

FATHER DAVIS: . . . to play a trick on time . . .

YOUNG PRIEST: Father, who art in heaven, hallowed . . .
hallowed be . . . thy . . .
> *(FATHER DAVIS starts opening the top snaps on the YOUNG PRIEST's cassock.)*

FATHER DAVIS: Shhhhh-shhh-shhh-shhh-shhhhhh.
> *(He slips his hand inside the YOUNG PRIEST's cassock. The YOUNG PRIEST leans back to push him away but traps himself deeper into FATHER DAVIS's erotic embrace.)*

YOUNG PRIEST: Hail Holy Queen, mother . . .

FATHER DAVIS: Let me . . .

YOUNG PRIEST: To thee do we cry poor banished . . .

FATHER DAVIS: Please . . . (LET ME . . .)
> *(FATHER DAVIS grasps the shoulder fabric of the YOUNG PRIEST's cassock.)*

YOUNG PRIEST: Please . . .

FATHER DAVIS: Please . . .

YOUNG PRIEST: Please . . .

FATHER DAVIS: Please . . .

YOUNG PRIEST: Please, PLEASE . . . (YES.)

FATHER DAVIS: Please.
> *(A shimmering sound as the YOUNG PRIEST bolts through the snaps of his cassock and emerges, like a butterfly from its cocoon, as WILL the male prostitute. FATHER DAVIS is left grasping an empty cassock.)*

WILL: So? You feel better now? Nothing to be ashamed of. Like being married. Makes me wanna . . . makes me wanna call you, like, I'm ashamed to say it . . . *(WILL embraces FATHER DAVIS from behind, then curls about him like a snake.)* Daaaarling. Always wanted to use that word. You passed out in ecstasy? What's the story? Talk to me. Shit. *(Sing-song, cajoling.)* Whatsamatta? You saaaad? *(Kisses his ear.)* Hey, Father. It's your pal, Willie. *(Scared.)* Say I love you again. I won't let you go. Say it. Say it for me. Why not? You're mean.

FATHER DAVIS: I love you.

WILL: Good. Take a drag. Go ahead.

FATHER DAVIS: No thanks.

WILL: How about a foot rub?

FATHER DAVIS: You're a good kid . . .

    (WILL jumps into his jeans, removes a money clip from a pocket.)

WILL: I'll go get you some coffee—black with sugar.

FATHER DAVIS: Do me a favor and . . .

WILL: Look what I got for you. A money clip. Solid silver.

FATHER DAVIS: Where'd you get that?

WILL: Bought it in a store. Not really.

FATHER DAVIS: Go for a walk.

WILL: You always make me feel guilty after.

FATHER DAVIS: You helped me, a lot.

WILL: Glad you know it.

FATHER DAVIS: Now I have to tell you something.

    (WILL sees it coming.)

WILL: Uh-uh. (NO.)

FATHER DAVIS: Can't do this anymore. Can't . . .

WILL: *(Panicking.)* What'ya think I do it for?

FATHER DAVIS: *(Overlap.)* Shhhh, now don't . . .

WILL: Didn't put out for you to tell me I'm some devil.

FATHER DAVIS: I can't say mass.

WILL: Because of me?

FATHER DAVIS: I lose my state of grace whenever we . . .

WILL: You're the one I do it for. It ain't for me.

FATHER DAVIS: Good then. You won't miss it.

WILL: No.

FATHER DAVIS: If you cared about me you would help me stop.

WILL: *(Pleading.)* We can stop. No more. No more.

FATHER DAVIS: You can't come around again.

WILL: Don't tell me that. No. Please, Father. I'm beggin' ya, I'm beggin' ya. Don't do that to me. I really love ya, really love ya, really.

FATHER DAVIS: My life doesn't . . .

WILL: Then leave it. It's makin' ya sick anyway. I'll support ya. Sure. I'll be a waiter. Maitre de. Pastry chef. I'll go to cooking school. Chefs make money.

FATHER DAVIS: I am no good.

WILL: I'm good for the two of us.

FATHER DAVIS: You don't know.

WILL: You don't know. I would work. I would be faithful. I would never leave you, never, never, never. We'll get wedding bands.

(FATHER DAVIS laughs lovingly but it inflames WILL.)

WILL: DON'T LAUGH AT ME!

FATHER DAVIS: You worry me.

WILL: I was never willing to give up so much for anyone in my life as I am for you.

FATHER DAVIS: You sweet kid, what'll you be giving up? It's I who'll be giving up my work, God.

WILL: Well I can't be God. So what do I get for my trouble?

FATHER DAVIS: Now don't try to hurt me.

WILL: I thought you were more than just some John. I wind up with nothing from them, nothing from you. What does that make you? Any different from them?

FATHER DAVIS: Yes. Because I loved you.

WILL: Like it's past tense? So where does it leave me now? I'm shit again.

FATHER DAVIS: Oh, c'mon.

WILL: What is it with you educated people? You go for little broken-down guys like me then dump us because we ain't good enough, we ain't old enough, we ain't smart enough.

FATHER DAVIS: Not true.

WILL: Why don't you go after people you'd be willing to give up your life for?

FATHER DAVIS: I already gave up my life.

WILL: Oh, to God. *(He opens his arms and screams to heaven.)* HEY GOD. HE JUST CHEATED ON YOU AGAIN. It'd be different if I was some college graduate.

FATHER DAVIS: I'd have to do this with anyone.

WILL: Do what? Do what? You said you loved me. "I love you." You said it twice . . .

FATHER DAVIS: I abused you.

WILL: Posh. I was after you from the minute I saw you.

FATHER DAVIS: Can't see you anymore.

WILL: 'Cause I'm your sin? That's all I been to you? Your sin boy? *(WILL grabs the TV remote as if it were a gun.)*

FATHER DAVIS: Willie, go for a walk.

WILL: I would have died for you. Killed for you. (*WILL points the remote.)* You fuck! YOU FUUUUCCCCKKKK! *(And zaps FATHER DAVIS into invisibility.)*

(Blackout except for the green television beam that strikes WILL's body. He remains frozen there in that green light. A light on old Father Rosetti asleep in a chair. His VCR is playing the opera Tosca *at a very low volume. The little dinner bell starts ringing on its own quite madly. In frustration, the bell actually speaks:)*

THE DINNER BELL (VOICE-OVER): Angelino, Angelino, Angelino. Little angel of the little roses. Wake up, Angelino, wake up, wake up, wake up. Terrible, terrible, terrible. Terrible!

THE SEALING OF CEIL

By Glenn Alterman

It is evening. MIKE and CEIL are sitting at the kitchen table intensely engaged in conversation. Moonlight shines in through some cracks in the closed blinds. MIKE is cutting a bagel with a very sharp knife.

CEIL: A murder, here?!

MIKE: Yeah!

CEIL: When?

MIKE: Yesterday.

CEIL: Ya kiddin'?!

MIKE: Swear to God.

CEIL: Who?

MIKE: Apartment 3B.

CEIL: Lady with the poodle?

MIKE: Yeah, her, the blonde with the hot pants.

CEIL: When?

MIKE: Middle of the day.

CEIL: I was here.

MIKE: Cops came . . .

CEIL: I was home.

MIKE: . . . took her body away.

CEIL: Didn't hear a thing.

MIKE: Bim-bam-boom!

CEIL: Musta been asleep.

MIKE: One-two-three!

CEIL: Really?

MIKE: Carlos said there was blood all over the place.

CEIL: Blood?!

MIKE: And that her hand . . .

CEIL: Yeah?

MIKE: . . . her right hand was cut off at the wrist.

CEIL: Cut?

MIKE: Severed, cut, yeah! *(MIKE puts the knife down.)*

CEIL: He said that?

MIKE: That's what he said. Said they couldn't find it at first.

CEIL: What, her hand?

MIKE: Was under the bed.

CEIL: Really?

MIKE: The poodle was playing with it.

CEIL: Her dog . . . ?

MIKE: . . . had her hand in his mouth, yeah.

CEIL: No!

MIKE: Wouldn't let go.

CEIL: No!!

MIKE: Cops tried getting it . . .

CEIL: Yeah?

MIKE: . . . but I guess the dog thought it was a game.

CEIL: What kina game?

MIKE: Tug-a-war I guess. Musta thought they were playing with him.

CEIL: The cops?

MIKE: Back and forth.

CEIL: With the dog?

MIKE: *(Annoyed.)* Tug-a-war, I'm telling you!

CEIL: Poor thing.

MIKE: Musta been hungry.

CEIL: What?

MIKE: His mistress is murdered, lotta blood, and here was the hand that feeds it.

CEIL: *(Realizing, touched.)* The dog just wanted to be fed.

MIKE: *(In her face.)* That's what I just said!

CEIL: *(Walking away, to herself, upset.)* Musta been screams . . .

MIKE: You never listen.

CEIL: . . . cries for help.

MIKE: Ceil? S'the toilet work?

CEIL: What?

MIKE: Toilet, the toilet, does it work?!

CEIL: Yeah.

MIKE: So he fixed it?

CEIL: Carlos? Yeah, yeah, yesterday.

MIKE: Finally. *(MIKE starts to leave.)*

CEIL: Where you goin'?

MIKE: To take a leak.

CEIL: Don't leave.

MIKE: Why not?

CEIL: I'm scared.

MIKE: Of what?

CEIL: There's a murderer loose!

MIKE: So lock the door.

CEIL: Mike, that girl's dead.

MIKE: So, s'not like you knew her?

CEIL: But I did.

MIKE: You knew her?

CEIL: Yeah.

MIKE: The girl in 3B?

CEIL: Yes.

MIKE: What, hello and good-bye in the hallway?

CEIL: No, no, we were friends.

MIKE: Friends?

CEIL: Her name was Fran, we talked all the time.

MIKE: You talked to her?

CEIL: Yeah?

MIKE: Where?

CEIL: Here.

MIKE: You had her here?

CEIL: Yeah.

MIKE: In our house?

CEIL: Yes.

MIKE: *(Getting angrier.)* I don't fuckin' believe this!

CEIL: What?

MIKE: I go to work, bust my chops, and she has tea with hookers!

CEIL: She was not a hooker.

MIKE: Sure she was.

CEIL: She was a social worker.

MIKE: Yeah, very social, I'm sure. Carlos said the downstairs door was like a nonstop turnstile.

CEIL: She was nice.

MIKE: Well now she's nice and dead! I don't fuckin' believe you! *(Going over to her.)* You never talked to her, understand?

CEIL: But I did.

MIKE: *(In her face.)* Anybody asks, wants to know, you never knew her!

CEIL: But I . . .

MIKE: Never!

CEIL: *(Softly.)* All right.

MIKE: We don't need nobody butting into our business. *(SHE looks at him. HE starts to go)* Now lock the door. *(SHE doesn't move.)* Lock—the—door!

CEIL: *(She watches him leave, then goes to the door. Softly mimicking him to herself.)* "Lock the door. Lock the door." *(SHE locks the door, puts the chain on.)* Poor girl. *(Suddenly there's knocking on the other side of the door. CEIL backs away, doesn't say anything. Knocking again. Softly.)* Who's there? *(No answer. Knocking. A little louder.)* Who is it?

VOICE: *(Whispering from the other side of the door.)* Me.

CEIL: Who? *(No answer, then.)* Who is it?

VOICE: Me . . . *(A beat, a loud whisper.)* . . . the murderer.

CEIL: Go away!

VOICE: *(A seductive whisper.)* Let me in.

    (CEIL picks up the knife from the table, holds it tightly, freezes.)

CEIL: Go away! GO WAY!

    (Blackout.)

I want the actor to be good. I look for the actor who knows what he's doing, is professional. You want to feel the actor knows what the material is about. I really hate when an actor comes in, is introduced to the director, and seems befuddled. It's a profession, a business. A lot of young actors just think it's art.

Pat McCorkle, casting director

Chapter 8

26 TIPS FOR
COLD READING MONOLOGUES

I look for an actor who makes me forget that I'm watching an audition! The actor should be fully involved in his character without projecting that he or she is conscious of being watched.

Diane Heery, casting director

Sometimes in a theater audition, the casting director will give an actor a monologue from the play to read cold. Also, I've been hearing that many independent film directors are now asking actors to cold read monologues as part of their first audition. If the director likes what he sees, he then gives the actor sides from the script to audition with. Since cold reading monologues is very different from cold reading plays and screenplays, I've included this chapter on the best ways to cold read monologues for auditions.

These are monologues that are given to you at an audition. This is different from the monologues that actors prepare before going to auditions. Rather than reading with you from a scene, some casting directors want to get a sense of your ability to make quick choices and personalize new material. Don't be surprised if they hand you a monologue and say

"Go take a look at it for a few minutes and come back in and read."

1. If you're given time to go out in the waiting area, read through the material quickly but thoroughly. Don't just scan it, try to absorb as much as you can. Breathe, focus, read. Read through the entire monologue, allow yourself to be entertained, to understand it. Leave yourself open to all information during this first meeting with the material.

2. After your initial read, read through the monologue again. Get a sense of the story of the monologue, what the playwright is trying to say. Determine what the emotional state of your character is. What is your character feeling at this place in time? During the course of the monologue, your character's emotions may change. Make sure you follow the tide of the emotions in the piece. Use your own feelings: personalize and substitute.

3. Mine the material for any humor. You'd be amazed how often there are glimpses of humor in even the darkest material. Adding humor helps to make even the most grim material more accessible. But don't add humor when it doesn't exist; always be truthful to the material.

4. Be sure you understand what the character's objective (intention) is. Throughout this book, we've been dealing with intentions, so hopefully by now you can make clear, strong choices.

5. Ask yourself, "Why is the character saying all this?" You must make a choice as to why the character is saying these words at this time.

6. Harness your nervous energy. Being nervous before an audition is a good thing. There is an energy that comes with

nerves that, if utilized, can be very exciting. Using that energy should be part of your preparation. Brando supposedly did push-ups every night before going out onstage to perform. Some actors run in place before going in, while others sit and breathe deeply to focus their nerves.

7. Never start off your auditions with questions like "Can I use you (as the other character)?" (the answer is generally no), or "Do you prefer if I stand or sit?" Hopefully you've decided whether to stand or sit while preparing in the waiting area.

8. Determine who your character is talking to. It's always helpful if you can use someone from your real life as the imaginary person rather than an abstraction. If no one comes to mind, then use your imagination. If you decide that the imaginary person is a young child or a very short person, where you'd normally look down, adjust your gaze accordingly, but keep it at a level where the auditors can see your eyes. Also determine out how close or far from you the other character is. Are you sitting opposite him in a restaurant, or is he at the other end of the room?

9. Decide how your character feels about the imaginary person. Does your character like, love, or hate this other person? Most important, does your character and the imaginary character have a close relationship or do they barely know each other? Are they perhaps related?

10. Make the auditors believe that you are truly communicating to another person (even though there is no one actually there). Most actors when rehearsing their monologue (and at the actual audition) generally pay little attention to the imaginary person that they're talking to. Perhaps they pick a spot on the back wall and talk to it. They've never really investigated what it would be like to actually

say those words to a real person (hopefully someone from their real lives).

Think about how a conversation in real life goes and pace your monologue accordingly. In real life when we are communicating with another person, imaginary arrows carry our words and thoughts from ourselves to that other person. These arrows communicate information as well as our intentions. When these arrows hit the mark, the other person understands what we are trying to say. At this point in the conversation, the other person responds: He might say something, or else a look in his eyes lets us know "he got it." After we notice that our listener has gotten the point, we continue with the conversation, going on to our next idea. How the other person responds, the look in his eyes when he got it, will flavor what we say next. Generally, this whole process occurs quite quickly, so we don't even notice or think about it. This circle of communication is ongoing between you and your listener.

This is an important concept to understand when doing a monologue for an audition. The more you observe and directly relate to your imaginary person, the more effective and dynamic your monologue will be. Unless you give the impression that you're actually speaking to another person, there will always be a slight flatness in your audition, no matter how good an actor you are. At best you'll give the impression that you're giving a speech, which is different from a monologue.

11. Establish where the imaginary person is and don't wander from that spot during the audition. Actors often forget where they originally set their imaginary person and change their focus during the audition. This is confusing to the auditors.

12. Some actors glue their eyes to the imaginary person in their scene. They stare nonstop, for the entire audition. This doesn't look realistic. Think of how you are in life. Very rarely will you lock eyes with someone you're talking to for an entire two minutes, even if it's an intense conversation. Every once in a while you'll look away—to gather your thoughts, notice something, or break the tension. Remember, when you're dealing with imaginary characters in your monologues, they will react to things that you're saying to them. The way that they react will affect how you say what you say and how (and when) you'll look at them.

13. Don't try to blow the auditors out of the water with over-the-top, explosive emotions. Sometimes, material simply done is far more effective than screaming, crying, and jumping up and down. Of course if the material requires heightened emotions and high energy, try to connect, but don't go overboard. You don't want to push or become overwrought.

14. When the monologue your auditioning with is from a Shakespearean play, it's best to try to play it realistically. Actors sometimes spend a great deal of their audition playing only the iambic pentameter or the rhymes. You don't need to play the poetry in the monologue; it's there. Go for the character and what he wants.

15. Be careful about upward inflections at the end of your sentences. Actors, sometimes feeling nervous, will end their sentences with an upward inflection, which makes their sentences sound like questions rather than statements. Make sure that there is a period at the end of every one of your sentences.

16. If you're in a casting director's or agent's office, be aware of the room and adjust your read to the space. You

shouldn't scream or run all over the place even if the material calls for it. Remember, it's an office, and business is going on; indicate the qualities called for without taking it too far. Adjust your volume to the playing area you're working in.

17. Always save a little for yourself. The material may be highly charged, but you must always remain grounded in yourself. Actors sometimes feel that exposing their raw emotions will be more effective. You must always be in control of yourself and the material.

18. When you're performing your monologue for a cold-read audition, everything you say and do is being observed. Where you focus your gaze as well as how you move (or don't) is all part of the performance. I've seen actors perform large chunks of their monologue with their eyes staring directly down at the script or, even worse, at the floor. Your body is being observed too. Even if you're seated, your body language should express what the character is going through. Many actors do monologues at their auditions as talking heads: everything from the neck down is dead. What's expected from you is a total performance, body included.

19. The first and last lines at monologue auditions are the most important. It's how the auditors first experience your work and how you leave them. By having a strong prebeat, you can have a great opening moment. If you're truthful throughout the ride of the monologue, it should land you honestly on the last line. Don't push at the end by adding an exclamation point for effect: it's counterproductive (unless the material calls for it).

20. Don't work too hard; try to enjoy the audition. If you enjoy what you're doing, then the auditors will enjoy it too. Because there isn't another actor to play off, actors

sometimes overcompensate by overplaying the material. Stay truthful. I always recommend that actors go off in a corner and read the monologue a few times before the actual audition. At first say the words softly, and then if possible (and appropriate), do it at full voice. But don't do it full out; save that for the audition.

21. Try not to pay too much attention to those negative voices in your head during an audition. One of the things my students constantly deal with is that internal nagging, self-critical voice. There you are trying to perform your monologue at the audition, but in the back of your mind, a voice says, "That's not good enough," "You're not talented," "Too slow," "Nobody will believe you," and on and on. This voice can deplete your energy and sabotage your work. It unfocuses your concentration. It makes you miserable. You must learn to come to terms with the self-critical voice and not allow it to throw you off track, especially under the pressure of an audition where it tends to get very loud sometimes.

22. Always take a beat after you've finished the monologue and say thank you. It's a way of letting them know that you're through with the work you've done on the material.

23. Be sensitive to wasting the auditors' time at the audition. It's not professional to chat up the auditors before or after your monologue. Some actors mistakenly believe that by ingratiating themselves after the audition, they'll somehow win points. The auditors have a lot of work to do in a very short period of time. The actor who monopolizes their time in conversation wastes their time; time that they could be using to audition other actors.

Be considerate, be succinct. If they want to chat with you, of course you should be gracious, professional, and accessible. Generally, when they chat with you after an audition, it's because they like what they saw and want to know more about you.

24. When you're through with the audition don't ask, "Was that what you were looking for?" You want to create the impression at the audition that this is how you see the material and wanted to play it.

25. Don't comment on how well you felt the monologue went or look at them for approval. Their perception of your audition may be very different from yours.

26. If they give you an adjustment to make with the monologue, try to take it and make it work. Don't question or argue with them about interpretation.

Chapter 9

ANALYSIS OF
COLD READING MONOLOGUES

I look for strong choices. It takes a while to see if someone is a yes, but the no is instantaneous. I look for someone who comes into the room and heats it up. And for some reason, that usually happens more often with women. Men are, by and large, more closed.

Stuart Howard, casting director

What follows are monologues for you to work on and some ideas of how you might approach this material at a cold-read monologue audition.

There is very little time for actors to make strong choices when that they're handed material of any kind at a cold-read audition. In the analysis sections are some areas where you may want to focus your attention. Anyone can just read the words in a scene. Unfortunately, many actors do that: just "read" material, in a somewhat detached manner. They color words and fake emotions. You want to find ways to connect to the material, to discover how it personally resonates for you. You always want to make the story on that page *your* story.

SEAGULLS ON SULLIVAN STREET

By Anastasia Traina

Lights up in a cozy neighborhood bar. It is nearly empty. Pete sits eating olives out of his martini. Alex the bartender wipes down the bar. LOUIE, who has a hearing problem that causes him to talk like he's retarded, returns from the bathroom and sits next to Pete.

LOUIE: It's a sad, sad story. I don't know if I could go into it. The pain . . . Alex, may I have a glass of water, please?
   (ALEX hands him a glass of water.)

LOUIE: Thanks. *(LOUIE drinks down the glass in one gulp.)* . . . Her name was Annabella, Annabelly Jelly. And I loved her. I can't tell you how deep was my love. She was everything to me . . . she was my best friend, my second self, my soul mate. We'd take these long, long walks and sit over by the piers and we just watch the sun go down . . . We stay until the daytime turned into nighttime, we didn't care. I could tell her things I never even told my mother. And she had an unusual beauty too. Like she had one blue eye and one black. And, and her hair was the color of wheat in the fall time . . . She was beautiful. Everything about her was beautiful even her lumpy belly was beautiful. She was, she was . . . she was jiggly—She was not fat. She had cancer lumps— *(Louie starts to cry.)* She didn't die of cancer. For pete sakes. It wasn't cancer or any other deadly disease that killed her . . . She was murdered. Murdered in cold blood. *(Silence.)* It happened on a Tuesday, two weeks ago . . . It was a drizzly day out and we were having our morning stroll. We were standing at the corner of Seventy-third Street, waiting for the light to turn green so that we could continue . . . So Annabella

Jelly is standing just in the street, very near the curb . . . and I'm standing on the curb, daydreaming like but not really . . . I was thinking, just thinking, about . . . "How lucky I am that I have Annabella Jelly! How I love her and she loves me. How everything seems sunny and bright now that she's in my life. And how I'm the luckiest man alive . . . " When out of nowhere, this taxi appears, crack-brain really, doing like a hundred on a city street, no less . . . So, so this crackbrain and a half, goes whizzing by me so, so fast, like faster then the Japanese shinkansen bullet train. Like one hundred and sixty-two miles an hour, that's about how fast he was probably going. He doesn't even pause, he just keeps on speeding and speeding, down the street not stopping for any red lights at all . . . And the next thing I know, Annabella Jelly is lying dead in the filthy gutter with her beautiful head smashed worse than, well . . . jelly, really . . . And I'm standing there, numb re-ally . . . Just standing there, holding on to her. Just holdin' on . . . No, her leash, her bloody leash. It was drippin' in blood and tiny mangled bits of hairs and skin— She wasn't a fucking dog. She was a Siberian husky, and she was a real survivor—

COLD-READING BREAKDOWN OF SEAGULLS ON SULLIVAN STREET

Refer to chapter 2, "48 Basic Requirements for All Cold Readings," as well as the tips in the last chapter on cold read-ing of monologues.

1. What is Louie's intention (objective)? What does he want from Pete by telling him this story? What does he hope to get by sharing this tale about Annabella? Why is he telling Pete this story?

2. What happened the moment before? He's just come back from the bathroom, but what has prompted him to begin this story now? It seems like it's a continuation of something that he started before going to the bathroom. It's always helpful for you to give yourself a prebeat, a moment before for the audition. It's a way of launching into the scene or monologue rather than just relying on the words in the first line.

3. What is his emotional state? Here Louie is clear. When he refers to the story he mentions "The pain . . ." Obviously he is suffering. Again, your preparation is key here. You must find a strong moment before. The monologue is a way for Louie to vent his feelings of grief.

4. What is his relationship to the imaginary person? Who is the imaginary person in this monologue? Because it's just a monologue you have to make assumptions about Louie and Pete's relationship. You might assume that because Louie is sharing his intense feelings with Peter they are close. Or it might just be that universal closeness that bartenders sometimes have with their regular customers.

5. Where is he? We are told specifically that he is in a bar. Not just any bar, but a "cozy, neighborhood bar." The bar is "nearly empty." It feels like an intimate setting for Louie to express his grief. There is a comfortableness that we have in our neighborhood bar, a familiarity we have with our regular bartenders.

THE TITLE OF THE PIECE

Often at the cold-read audition, you are given just the monologue, or the sides, not the entire play or screenplay. The title is your starting place. With some material, be it a play, screenplay, or TV script, the title can provide a big clue about the material's content. Remember, in the limited time you have, you're always looking for first impressions. What impression does the title *Seagulls on Sullivan Street* give you? How can that first impression help you connect with the monologue?

Tennessee Williams, like most playwrights, named his plays very carefully. *Sweet Bird of Youth, A Streetcar Named Desire,* and *The Glass Menagerie* are all poetic and informative titles. They tell us something about the stories of the plays, the mood. The same is true for Eugene O'Neil, such as *Long Day's Journey into Night* and *Desire under the Elms.*

TV series titles, such as *Sex in the City, Charlie's Angels, The Twilight Zone,* or *Friends,* can also give you clues about the content.

YOUR CHARACTER'S NAME

Look at your character's name. Do you get any impression from the name *Louie*? If he was called Louis, perhaps you'd get a different impression. Louie is a regular guy. Does the way he speak, his dialogue, seem in sync with his name?

Playwrights and screenwriters choose their characters' names carefully; it is yet another small clue. There are some playwrights who have fun with their characters' names. They give them names that are characteristic of who they are. George Bernard Shaw, Tennessee Williams, and Edward Albee are playwrights who have written plays where names indicate something about the characters.

GETTING THE GIST OF THE STORY

You want to read through the material slowly, getting the gist of what the story is about. As actors we are storytellers. Our job is to interpret the story and help realize it on the stage. What's happening in the monologue? You need to understand what the story is about. It's difficult to play a character if you don't know where he fits into the story being told. With a monologue such as this one, it may be difficult to know much about the rest of the play. Use your imagination and see if you can come up with a context for the monologue. In this monologue, Louie is telling the story of his love for his Annabella. We don't know much about the rest of the play, so we have to use our imagination and make choices as to where this story about Annabella might fit into the play.

HOW DOES THE CHARACTER SPEAK?

Notice how the character speaks—not only what he says, but his vocabulary, his choice of words, his tone, his ideas. These can give you indications of the type of person he is. Is he well spoken, educated? Is he a blue-collar guy? Language is a great indicator of who we are. The same is true of characters in a play. Be aware of the character's choice of words, his colloquial expressions, the way the character turns a phrase. Louie says, "So Annabella Jelly is standing just in the street, very near the curb . . . and I'm standing on the curb, daydreaming like but not really . . . I was thinking, just thinking, about . . . 'How lucky I am that I have Annabella Jelly.'" What kind of person do you feel he is? See if you can identify with him, and make your choices on how you want to play him in the monologue.

THE SUBJECT OF THE PIECE

What is he (and the playwright) talking about? What are they trying to say? What point are they trying to make in telling their story. It comes down to what Louie's point is. He says, "Her name was Annabella, Annabelly Jelly. And I loved her. I can't tell you how deep was my love. She was everything to me . . . she was my best friend, my second self, my soul mate. We'd take these long, long walks and sit over by the piers and we just watch the sun go down . . . We stay until the daytime turned into nighttime, we didn't care. I could tell her things I never even told my mother." This is a tale of love and mourning. How you choose to play that at the audition should be based on your own connection to these themes.

THE TONE AND THE MOOD OF THE SCENE

You want to capture the mood, tone, and flavor of a scene in your audition. Aside from the comedic or dramatic aspects, there are underlying qualities that may permeate the material. Generally, the writing of Christopher Durang's plays are different in style from, say, David Mamet's.

I remember years ago I went to an early reading of Nicky Silver's dark comedy *Pterodactyls*. It was at a prestigious theater in New York with a very good cast and director. The reading went pretty badly because the company and the director had not understood the style (and mood) of the play. Rhythms were off, and the humor was lost. It wasn't until the play opened a year later that I realized how funny the play really was.

WHAT IS THE CHARACTER DOING?

During this monologue, Louie asks Alex for a glass of water, and "Louie drinks down the glass in one gulp." That action gives us a small indication of his emotional state. If he sipped it slowly, we'd feel differently. By the way, you don't need to pantomime a character's actions at an audition. A simple indication of what he's doing is enough. Decide what actions will best reflect Louie's emotional state.

WHY IS HE TELLING THIS TALE AT THIS TIME?

One of the important given circumstances is why the character is telling a story at this moment in time. If you don't feel there is enough information in the play itself, you must use your imagination and create reasons.

In this monologue we discover how much Louie cared for his Annabella Jelly. Who Annabella is we learn in the surprise ending of the piece. This is a story about a man who deeply loved his dog who died. This is a monologue that deals with grief, mourning.

Suppose you don't care for dogs? Then you have to substitute whatever you need to make this material work for you. Perhaps you're a cat person. Or maybe you can relate better to the material if you imagine Annabella to be a child. As always, make this story your own.

ELIZABETH (FROM *SIXTY SECONDS TO SHINE: 101 ORIGINAL ONE-MINUTE MONOLOGUES*)

By Glenn Alterman

Seriocomedic. Elizabeth is in her twenties or thirties. She recalls the last time she saw her boss.

You arrogant bastard, no wonder no one likes you! That's what I should have said. But I didn't, I just thought it. You don't say things like that to him, not him, no. Not unless you want to be fired. But I was this close, this close! He told me I had to work again all weekend. Even though I'd just told him, I had plans, family. But he just sneered, said he was sorry, he needed me. So I stormed out of there. Said, "Fine, sure, OK!" Sat at my desk and fumed, I was furious! And so I was just about to call you, to cancel, when I heard like a crash, then a moan. I got up, went to his door, knocked; nothing. Then I heard another moan, went inside, saw him lying there on the floor. He looked terrible, Terry. Pale, pasty. I bent down, didn't know what to say. He seemed so frightened, fragile. He tried to touch my face with his hand. It was like a really tender moment. And then I held him. And then—then he died, yeah, right there in my arms. I was the last person he ever saw. Me, who he always humiliated, tormented, tortured. There he was, Terry, dead in my arms. And he looked so pathetic.

Then I got up, went over, and sat in his chair; his big, brown chair. Looked around his office. Y'know I never noticed he but has a very nice office. Spacious, nice. And you know what I started to think about? Unemployment; unemployment, Terry. I wondered, if your boss dies in your arms, are you eligible? Then I wondered how much I'd get every week. And then, well then I called the police. And while waiting, I slowly began to swirl around in his chair. Just swirl around, watching the room go by. I just sat there, Terry, in his big, comfortable brown chair, smiling, happy, and swirling!

COLD READING OF ORIGINAL MONOLOGUES

In general, you won't be asked to read cold from an original monologue book. I've written many books of original monologues and have, on many occasions, asked actors to read new material for me before sending it off to the publishers. These reads are usually a cold read. I like to see how the material works without any preconceived ideas.

Also, when I'm working on new, original monologue material, I ask my professional students if they'd help me out by reading the material (cold) to see if it works. I know of many other writers that ask actors to read their plays and monologues for them, usually cold. There is a value to hearing how your material flies off the page.

Actors looking through monologue books (original and from plays) should always read the material out loud. First, you want to see if it appeals to you, and then read it aloud to see how it feels to say the words. Make sure it plays as well as it looks on the page. You will be performing these pieces at auditions.

COLD-READING BREAKDOWN OF ELIZABETH

Decide what the given circumstances are.

WHAT IS THIS MONOLOGUE ABOUT?

In this monologue, Elizabeth is sharing the story of how her boss died (in her arms). The profound effect that this had on Elizabeth is revealed in the way she expresses herself as she tells the story.

One question you always want to ask yourself when doing a past-tense monologue is, "How long ago did this story happen?" If there is no clear indication in the text, then you should go with a more dramatic choice. What do you think Elizabeth's emotional state would be if this happened to her boss last month? What do you think her emotional state would be to if it happened to him half an hour ago? Obviously, half an hour ago is a more dramatic choice. By going for that, you will probably be more engaged by the material and (hopefully) so will the auditors watching your audition.

WHO IS THE CHARACTER?

In original monologues such as this one, what you see is what you get. The monologue is complete. There is no play to read where you can find clues about your character. In one way, this makes your job easier.

You can begin to make assumptions about Elizabeth's character by noticing the following:

- the way she tells her story
- her emotional state and how it changes through the piece
- her description of her relationship to her deceased boss
- the way she tell the story to Terry, the person she's talking to

The impression you might get is that she was intimidated by her boss. To some degree, he was somewhat abusive of her. Perhaps she needed the job (the money), so she tolerated his abuse. Your job is to find ways to personally identify with her situation. Have you ever had a boss (or teacher) who was intimidating? Try to connect with your feelings of frustration and/or fear and use them in the earlier part of the monologue.

WHERE IS THE CHARACTER?

Since the setting of the monologue is not revealed in the piece, you must choose a location (from your real life) where you might be telling this story to Terry. Perhaps you're at your friend Terry's house. Perhaps Terry is a relative, and you're telling her this story in a coffee shop. Use your imagination based on the impressions you got when you originally read the monologue.

Setting a monologue in a real place from your real life is another way of grounding yourself in the material and making it real for yourself.

WHEN DOES THIS STORY TAKE PLACE?

The story is being told in the present, but the event Elizabeth describes happened earlier. Hopefully, the images in the monologue will emotionally engage you enough to make the story come to life in the present. You want to avoid a past-tense, just "reporting" tone. Let the images move you and put the story in the present tense, as if it were happening right now. The more you can make it alive now the better your audition will be both for you and for the auditors.

WHAT TIME OF YEAR IS IT? WHAT TIME OF DAY OR NIGHT?

Since the time of year and day is not given in the monologue, you need to add these elements to the story from your personal life. Telling a friend a story on a cold February day at three in the morning will play differently than a story being told to a friend on a hot July afternoon. These add-ons from your own life will make the material more personal.

WHAT IS THE CHARACTER DOING?

Since there is no indication of what she's doing in the monologue, you can create behavior that fits the character. She may be seated during the story or standing or sitting than standing.

If you decide she's to remain seated during the entire story, how she sits is important. You can sit in a chair in many different ways. You can nervously fidget with the arms of the chair while telling the story, or you can tensely grip the chair's arms at emotional moments. If you decide she's standing, you must justify why she's standing. Perhaps you've picked a location where she could only be standing. Or perhaps she's so excited she has to stand.

WHAT DOES SHE WANT? WHY IS SHE TELLING THIS STORY?

Why do you think Elizabeth is telling this story to Terry? What do you think she wants? Acknowledgment? To share her joy? Deciding what Elizabeth's intention in telling this story is key to playing her. Make a strong decision and stick with it. You may be wrong, but a wrong decision is better than just reading the lines without any intention.

We tell people stories to get a response of some kind. Sometimes it's to get their sympathy. Sometimes it's to get a rise out of them, shock them. Sometimes it's just to share how ironic life is. We may be telling them the story to make them laugh, upset them, or get them to revolt against some injustice.

Determining why a character tells a story is like an engine for the actor. Not knowing why the character is telling the story will leave you babbling without any focus.

NOTICE THE "STATS"

In this original monologue, we are given the character's age range of twenties to thirties, and we're told right off the bat that this material is seriocomedic. From these two clues, we learn some valuable information about the material.

Just so you know, publishers generally ask the original monologue writer to include age ranges for all the monologues in a monologue book. It's one way that actors can see if material is in their age range. But many of these age-range stats are arbitrary. Even though an age range of twenties to thirties is given, there is no reason that a forty-year-old woman couldn't do this piece. See if anything in the material indicates a specific age that would prohibit you from doing it.

One thing I discourage is women playing men's parts. and vice versa. I know some people like to take on that challenge, but for me, when I create a woman, it comes from a different place than when I write a male role.

We're given a brief introduction, "Elizabeth recalls the last time she saw her boss." "The last time" could mean he went off on a vacation, but we soon learn that he died. The introductions in monologue books are usually written succinctly to indicate what the material is about so that the actor-reader can decide if he wants to work on the piece. Some subjects are offensive or just not of interest to actors, and they'll chose not to read the monologue that follows.

THE FIRST LINES

The first lines of a monologue are very important at an audition. Many casting directors say that, for them, those lines are the most important parts of the audition. The first lines generally indicate to a director if the actor has prepared properly or is just "reading" without any sense or commitment. Before you say that first word, make sure that you're prepped and ready to go. Since time is tight at the cold-read audition, you want to make strong choices and then find a way to personally connect to the material. You can't hope that as you continue reading, you'll "get into it."

Trying to wing it without preparation is, at best, risky. There's nothing worse than beginning an audition and then realizing you're really not into it, that you're just reading words on a page without any connection. It's a constant game of catch-up. Casting directors may see fifty or more people in a day. If you're not there at the top of the audition, you may lose their interest. They'll tune out and start thinking about something else.

The first line of this monologue is strong, ending with an exclamation point, "You arrogant bastard, no wonder no one likes you!" She is telling someone off in no uncertain terms. You want to meet that first moment emotionally as fully as you can. Again, preparation is key. You want to find something that will hurl you into the emotional place that Elizabeth is in.

The next line—"That's what I should have said"—indicates a quick change in mood. We realize that she's not as bold as we thought she was. You must take the transition and make it work for you.

Throughout this piece there are several changes in mood. We go from anger to fear (of her boss dying), to shock (his death), to discovery (of how nice his office and chair is), to release (that she is no longer imprisoned by an abusive boss). Emotional transitions are an actor's best friend at an audition. It allows you to show that you have the ability to change emotions on a dime, depending on what the character is saying and feeling.

Some actors start off on a strong note and, because of nerves or possibly misinterpretation, never let go of one emotion. It makes for an uninteresting audition. One of the secrets to cold reads—well, to all good acting—is to remain open, flexible, and focused. Sometimes material will veer in unexpected directions.

RELATIONSHIP TO THE IMAGINARY PERSON: WHO YOU'RE TALKING TO

One of the most important parts of any monologue audition, cold or otherwise, is the imaginary person you're talking to. One of the first questions a casting director will ask himself in these auditions is "Do I believe he's really talking to someone?" Monologues can be especially difficult because no one is there: You are talking to an imaginary person. Without having a particular person in mind, your audition will become unfocused. At best, you will just be making a speech. You must convince the auditors that you are really talking to someone.

You may get an idea of what Terry looks like from your imagination, or you can substitute someone from your real life, place her in front of you, and talk directly to her.

Whatever works best for you. If you decide that Terry is a friend or relative, you must also decide how close or intimate you are.

THE TELLING OF THE TALE

There is a way we all tell stories to listeners. From friends sharing exciting events, to people sharing secrets, to conversations in bars with strangers, we are all constantly telling people our stories. In your day-to-day life, notice how people tell you (and others) their stories. There is a certain drama involved in storytelling, a certain suspense. We build our stories in a certain way when communicating them. Everyone enjoys a good yarn. The secret to giving a good monologue audition, cold or otherwise, is knowing how you want to tell the story in a dramatic, effective way. It may be that your character has a need to communicate his story to relieve himself of some deep guilt, or that the character feels that he'll burst if he doesn't share some exciting news.

Have you figured out why Elizabeth is telling her story? What's so important that she feels the need to tell Terry now?

THE LAST LINE

There is nothing you should do, acting wise, at the end of the monologue. Hopefully, you've taken the journey of the piece in an honest way and have come to the completion in the same manner. But be aware, as I mentioned previously, many casting directors take special note of beginnings and endings of monologues. It's how you start the ride and how you end it. Many actors try to put an exclamation point on the last line just to be remembered. If the material indicates to you that you should be gentle at the end, then by all means, be gentle. In this monologue the last lines are: "And while waiting, I slowly began to swirl around in his chair. Just swirl around, watching the room go by. I just sat there, Terry, in his big, comfortable brown chair, smiling, happy, and swirling!"

The journey of the monologue ends with Elizabeth obviously overjoyed. It ends "smiling, happy, and swirling!" Notice the exclamation point after the last word. If you've honestly paved the way through the piece, it will pay off with a joyful landing on her last line.

Chapter 10

EXERCISES FOR
COLD READING MONOLOGUES

I look for sheer ability to act and also somebody who knows how to bring their own personality into a room and into their work. Auditions are a very strange thing. What I hope for all the time is that the actor walking in the door is the perfect person for the role. Many years ago when I first started working with Neil Simon, he told me that he had invited Marcia Mason to auditions one day. And at the end of the day, he said that he liked the same people that Marcia liked. And then Marcia said, "Now I understand. The actors pick you, you don't pick the actors." Sometimes an actor comes in and that particular magic happens, they "own the part."

When Kate Burton auditioned for Jake's Women, *she opened her mouth and the part came out. Neil was very enthusiastic, and we just asked her to keep reading well past what she had prepared. And the part just came out.*

Jay Binder, casting director

What follows are some monologues that you can practice to develop your cold-reading skills. Be sure to review the previous information on cold reading of monologues and the first couple of chapters on all the basics.

Find a monologue that you feel works for you. Read it carefully, gathering as much information as you can. Allow yourself about fifteen minutes to work on the monologue, and then read it aloud as if you were at an audition. Perhaps ask an actor friend to play the role of the casting director in a mock audition scenario.

Be sure to determine the given circumstances and then make active, personal choices for each monologue.

- What is this monologue about? Try to discover the world that this play or scene takes place in. What is the event in the monologue?

- Who is the character? You should get a feel for the character that you're playing. If you don't, you'll just be reading words from a script at your audition. You need to understand your character, identify with him. See where you can connect, use your imagination.

- What is the relationship between your character and the imaginary character(s)? You must always determine what the relationship is between your character and the person you're talking to. Do you like, love, or hate this person? Do you need them for something? Why are you talking to them?

- Where is the character? Determine where the monologue takes place. If it's not mentioned in the script then use your imagination.

- Does this monologue take place in the present, past, future? What time of year is it? What time of day or night?

- What is the character doing? Find playable actions that you can perform at the audition. Be careful not to bog yourself down with too many actions. Make it simple.

- What does he want? You must have a strong intention for every monologue you audition for. The intention is the driving force of the scene. It's the need, the goal of your character. In acting classes you're told to pick an active verb for your intention. It all comes down to what does your character want in that scene and how will he go about getting it?

- What is preventing him (the obstacle) from getting what he wants? Knowing (and playing) the intention and finding (and playing) the conflict is crucial to any scene. Obstacles come in all forms, from a character's insecurities or neuroses, to the other character in the scene doing something that prevents you from getting what you want. Bottom line, whatever impedes you from getting to your goal is the obstacle that your character is trying to overcome.

After you've worked on some of these monologues, feel free try them out at your next audition where a monologue is required.

MEREDITH (FROM *GOD IN BED*)

By Glenn Alterman

(An upset, angry tirade.) I hate them, that's all, just hate 'em! Way they walk, limp, bump into things. Never say they're sorry! No, too preoccupied with their own thoughts. And did you ever smell their breath? P.U.! Put your teeth back in, please! And they're always in a bad mood, always, haven't you noticed?! Constantly complaining about this or that. The world outside, their bed, their bones. How everything hurts! They're just one big pain—old people!

And they can't sleep, no! Up all night so they're tired all

the time. Can't eat, digest their food, go to the toilet. Constantly constipated! Have to eat barrels and barrels of prunes. I will never get that old, never! Not like that, no.

And all they ever talk about, all they "ever" talk about, is the past. The glorious past, the way it was, the goddamned good old days. Always backtracking.

And he falls, breaks a hip, so "you" have to take care of him. Give him his meals, find him his pills; his many, many bottles of pills. Which one, which time of day? Make sure he swallows, doesn't choke. *(Losing some momentum.)* And then you watch, you watch. As he slowly gives up, starts to fade. A little more today than yesterday. You can see it; can see it in his eyes. You're losing him. You tell him a joke, a story, anything. But he's stopped recognizing. He doesn't know you or anybody. You show him pictures, try to re . . .

Grandpa was so robust, remember? So alive, full of life! Always smiling. Strong, firm hands. Would throw us up in the air and catch us, remember? He took me to my first movie, did you know that? Was *Heidi, Heidi.* And I fell asleep in his lap. So safe. *(A beat, softly.)* I remember . . . Do you remember how he . . . ? The way he'd . . . That look he'd . . . ! Grandpa was so . . . I'll always . . . He was so . . . ! He was . . . He . . . was.

PROPOSAL (FROM *GLORY BOX*)

By Tim Miller

It was a day of judgmental Twinkies being smashed in my face. I was nine years old. I was walking down Russell Street with my friend, Scott; he was a second cousin of President Richard Nixon and we lived in Whittier, the president's hometown. So you can see, Republicans have been fucking with me for as long as I can remember. We walked, free-associating as young boys will do. We walked by a house that was widely regarded as the most tasteful in our neighborhood, much respected for its impressive series of ceramic elves decorating the winding walkway to the front door!

Scott said to me, "When I grow up, I'm going to marry that cute girl in our class, Gail Gardener, and we're gonna live in that house with the ceramic elves." Then Scott looked at me as if he thought he deserved a ninety-nine and a happy face on a spelling test.

This was a new subject, and I sensed that it meant trouble. I bought some time and walked silently along, my *Lost in Space* lunch box clanking against my leg. My *Lost in Space* lunch box filled with my favorite lunch. A sandwich, made with Wonder Bread, of course, and layers of delicious Jiffy smooth peanut butter and Welch's grape jelly with a generous crunchy handful of Fritos corn chips in-between. (Mmm, all that delicious sugar, oil, and salt! Everything a young American needs to grow strong.) Next to my thermos was a special treat: a Twinkie in its crisp, confident plastic wrapper.

I knew I was making a mistake before I even opened my mouth, "But, Scott, when I grow up, I want to marry you and live in the house with the ceramic elves!" He looked at me as if I suggested that we tap dance together to the moon.

"What! Boys can't get married to each other. Everybody knows that."

"Why not?"

"They just can't."

"Why?"

"Because."

"Because why?"

Clearly, logic wasn't working, so Scott pushed me hard with both hands, knocking me into the deep dusty ivy of my Congregationalist minister's front yard. We all knew rats lurked and prospered in the dark gnarly labyrinth of the ancient ivy. I drowned in the dirty green.

Scott jumped on me, looking around to see if anyone had heard me ask him to marry him, "Take it back! Say you don't want to marry me and live in the house with the elves!"

"I won't take it back!"

"Take it back, or I'll give you an Indian burn." He pinched my side hard and then grabbed my wrist with both hands and twisted in opposite directions. I screamed.

"Do you take it back?"

"I won't take it back!"

He Indian-burned my other wrist. I probably could have fought him off, I wasn't that much of a wuss, but part of me had longed for some kind of closeness with Scott ever since kindergarten. Being tortured by him would have to do. You've all been there. My lunch box had fallen open near my head, revealing the Twinkie in all its cellophane splendor. Scott got a horrible idea and grabbed the Twinkie in his little fist.

"Take it back or I'm going to jam this Twinkie in your throat and kill you!"

"I won't take it back!" The strength of my high-pitched voice surprised me. "When I grow up, I'm going to marry you and live in the house with the ceramic elves!"

A look of shock and frustration passed like bad weather across Scott's face. Scott shoved the Twinkie into my mouth and held his small dirty palm over my lips. I exploded with cellophane and Twinkie goo. Now, I knew that even more than climbing into boxes with lids, I knew kids weren't supposed to suck on cellophane. I took the warnings on the dry-cleaning bags seriously. I knew I'd reached my Twinkie limit, and I would have to take it back. Fortunately, my oldest brother had just taught me the week before a special trick. Whenever anyone is tormenting you and wanting you to be untrue to yourself and take something back, all you have to do is cross your fingers and put them behind your back. This erases it. In case you thought this stopped working in childhood, it didn't. It still works in adult life, especially around relationship issues! I quickly crossed my fingers behind my back.

"All right! I take it back." Scott got off of me. He looked so strange. He kicked me, grabbed his math book and banal Bonanza lunch box, and stormed off to school and the rest of his life filled with petty disappointments and three wives who would fear him. (Don't ask me how, I just know!)

I lay there on my back, pinned to the earth. Surrounded by primordial ivy dust and Twinkie. I pulled my crossed fingers from underneath my back and held them up to the sky. The crossing of those fingers negated my "I take it back!," my one triumph over his small tyranny. I held them up to the hot California sun as I repeated the words, they gathered steam inside me. "I will never take it back. I will never take it back. I will never take it back."

BETTY (FROM *GOD IN BED*)

By Glenn Alterman

(*Very upset.*) It's raining, I'm pissed, and you're depressed. Now if you want, if you really want, Tom, we can continue sitting here in the dark. We can do that sure, why not? We do it very well. We have become "experts" at sitting in the dark. I mean, why talk, right? Why bother talking when a look or a grunt will do? Well, how about this for an idea? How 'bout we try something unusual tonight; something we hardly ever do anymore? How about you and I, Tom, try to "talk"; talk Tom! You know, like one word following another? Who knows, might be fun? We might even have a feeling fly in here, some emotions might join the fray. Think you could handle it,

Tom; words, thoughts, feelings?! Be like a goddamned communication orgy here.

Tom, hey Tom, I'm talking to you! I am . . . *(A beat.)* You used to talk. Used to, remember? Talked all the time. Heard you loud and clear back in the bar that first time. Oh yeah, the first time we met, I couldn't shut you up. You talked a blue streak that night. Sweet things. Nice words. Compliments. *(Beat.)* Y'know, y'know, I feel sorry for you, Tom, I do. You're a sad, pathetic person. You're dead inside. So sit there in the dark, Tom, dead. I don't really care anymore. *(A beat.)* I'm leaving. I'm going now. I'm tired of talking. Tired of wondering if you're even listening; if you're even awake! —HEY ARE YOU AWAKE, TOM?!

I'm leaving, I'm going; good-bye. Please—don't get up. I can find my way in the dark, have been doing it . . . 'Sides why ruin a good Saturday night by turning on the light, right? I'll use my key, let myself out, just like always. *(A beat, softer.)* Look, I'll call ya, OK? Next Saturday. Same time, Tom? Seven? Seven? . . . I'll call ya, Tom. Yeah, . . . I'll call ya.

YOUNG GIRL (FROM *NEW YORK VALUES*)

By Penny Arcade

I climb out my window at night and I walk around in the dark. There's no room for my imagination in that house. Peasant Italians don't believe in imagination. They believe in work. Girls are supposed to work. Boys are the kings, girls are the slaves. I come home from school, I open the door, I step inside, and I skip six centuries. It's medieval Italy, and I'm a serf. Sometimes I stop cleaning and I read the dictionary.

I read the dictionary 'cause it's the only book in the house. That drives Ma crazy. Ma says it would be better if I was born strong instead of smart, but I love words. I collect them. Maybe because English isn't my first language, it feels like it's really mine. Maybe because peasant Italians only talk about misery, death, suffering, and the weather. English feels exotic and modern to me. It's not trailed by three thousand years of suffering and isolation like my mother's southern Italian dialect. It 's not just another language! It's another way of life! All right! I'll admit it! It's an escape.

Two words that never meant that much to me are Mommy and Daddy. These words seem more like titles, like mayor or officer or nurse. They don't have the same sense of possibility I find in other words in English. Everytime I say the word *Daddy*, I feel like a liar. Every time I say the word *Mommy*, it has a question mark.

I grew up in a factory town surrounded by rich suburbs.

Walking downtown meant walking through miles of tool and dye shops, the constant pounding of the ball-bearing factories. Later, when I heard walls of amps, it didn't mean much to me. The backbeat of rock and roll was pounded into me early. People who have heard of my hometown, New Britain, Connecticut, always say the same thing, "Oh, New Britain, girls from New Britain fuck." New Britain, Connecticut, New England mill town, New Britsky, Polish factory town, center of working-class intellectualism, exporting Stanley tools, Black and Decker, and bad girls.

CHLOE (FROM *GOD IN BED*)

By Glenn Alterman

After seeing Bob around town for years, Chloe finally has a date with him.

(Anxiously, nonstop, rambling.) It's all like predetermined, preordained, whatever you want to call it, Bob. Everyone knows it; ya learn it in Life 101. There are no accidents, no, none! Not even here, in small town U.S.A. We bump, melt, merge, whatever you want to call it, with people we are meant to meet, meant to meet! I believe that, I do. I mean think about it, just think about it, Bob; fact that you're here, I'm here, and we're both sitting in your car, front of my house; ready to go, night on the town, no accident, no-no-no. No mistake, none. Preordained. And I want you to know, want you to know, Bob, I was thrilled when you called last week. Thought oh my God, BOB, imagine, finally! After all these years, Bob! Not that I was sitting by the phone, no. I'm so busy these days at the library, nonstop, go-go-go; books back and forth; library lunacy. So you were really lucky to get me in, lucky I was even home. Luck, lucky, preordained. But it was certainly a surprise. I mean after all these years of seeing you at the supermarket, passing you on the street, seeing you drive by. Certainly a surprise. And now, here, the two of us, sitting in your car, waiting, waiting patiently, may I add, for you to put the key in the ignition so we can go somewhere and . . . *(Looking at him.)* So why don't you start the car? Car can't start by itself. We can't go anywhere just sitting here. *(SHE turns to her door.)*

Why'd you open my door? . . . Bob, Bob, you don't want me to leave, do you? I can't go. No Bob, no you don't understand, this is . . . This is a brand-new dress! This is our first . . . ! No, you don't understand. Bob, Bobby, Robert, this has all been—preordained!

YOUNG WOMAN (FROM *BAD REPUTATION*)

By Penny Arcade

When I was thirteen years old, kids my age, we'd go to the movies on Saturday, on Sundays. Sometimes we'd meet boys. Sometimes we go in the balcony and hold hands, sometimes we'd kiss. One Sunday I met this boy. He was sixteen. Something about him made me nervous. When he kissed me, I didn't like it. Later he held my wrist real hard and made me promise to meet him in the park the next night. I never showed up. Two weeks later my whole life changed.

Boys started driving by my house at night yelling things.

Boys would stop my brother and sister on their way home from elementary school and say, "I want to fuck your sister." Pretty soon no one would talk to me at school, pretty soon no one would sit with me in the cafeteria. Strange boys would wait for me after school.

At night I'd lay in my bed and watch the headlights of the cars move across my ceiling. It hurt so bad I couldn't cry. Sometimes it hurt so much that I would slap myself in the face till I cried, "I can't . . . I can't . . . I can't."

Then I would dream about the blonde boy from the other side of town, how he would rescue me, how he would save me, how he would champion me. One night I went down to the skating rink and I saw him, the blonde boy from the other side of town. I was wearing black eye makeup. I thought I was supposed to. He said, "Hey! Why do you have that shit on your eyes? You're too pretty for that! Go wash it off." And I went into the girls' room and I washed it off and when I came out he was gone. The next day I went to the other side of town where he hung out. He was glad to see me. We started to talk and for the first time he asked me about the boy from the movie theater. I trusted him. I started to tell him what happened and then . . . From around the corner, I saw him. The boy from the movie theater. He was walking towards us and he was yelling, "Hey little whore! What are you doing slutting on this side of town?" He walked right up to me and the blonde boy and he said, "What are you doing slutting on this side of town?" and the blonde boy turned to me and he said, "Is what he says about you true?" I burst into tears. I started running and I couldn't stop. The boy from the movie theater was yelling, "Look at the lying whore run! Run little whore! Run!"

After that I stopped going to school on time. After that I stopped going to school. After that I stopped coming home. After that I ran away. After that I got caught. After that I got put away. Two years later when I got out of reform school, everyone said I had a baby. I never had a baby. I never slept with anyone. I never had a baby. I never slept with anyone. I've never had a baby.

See, I never tell people more than three things, three bad things that have happened to me. Cuz I can't stand the look of pity in their eyes. I can't stand watching them do that fast arithmetic in their heads. I can't stand watching them shift their weight from foot to foot. It seems like time stands still waiting for that sigh to come out of their Cheerio mouth, that little "phew," that means "nothing like that could ever happen to me."

COLD READING A MONODRAMA

A monodrama is a one-person play. Aside from the obvious difference in length from audition and original monologues, a monodrama is a complete solo play. Some well-known monodramas include *The Belle of Amherst, Tru, Spic-orama, Mambo Mouth, The Search for Intelligent Life in the*

Universe, The Syringa Tree, Golda's Balcony, Bridge and Tunnel, and *Nine Parts of Desire.* Some of these solo shows, like *Golda's Balcony* and *The Belle of Amherst,* are composed of one story with the actor portraying many characters. Other monodramas, such as Eric Bogosian's *Fun House* and *Drugs, Sex, Rock and Roll,* are individual character monologues strung together with a theme of some kind.

Most of the previously mentioned rules that pertain to monologue cold reads apply to the monodrama. Generally, because of their length, if you're asked to audition for a monodrama, you'll be only given a section of the play to audition with.

Lanie Robertson's monodrama *God's Game* is a relatively short monodrama. Some monodramas can run from an hour to two hours. Here is an excerpt from his piece.

GOD'S GAME

By Lanie Robertson

SISTER, a nun in full habit, faces audience. She clutches a baseball bat in one hand, a softball in the other. She tosses the ball a few inches in the air above her palm and catches it, unconsciously. She does this several times. For a time, she doesn't move except for clutching the bat and tossing the ball. Now, she paces, nods, and smiles knowingly at the audience. Her pacing does not interfere with her gripping or tossing.

SISTER: Well, well, well. Just look at you! Just look at all of you! What a sorry-looking bunch of sniveling, snot-nosed, sanctimonious little sluts you really are! Well, you've done it again! Disgraced yourselves again!

(Confidently.) But this time . . . with a difference! This time . . . everybody knows it!

Not just me. Oh, no! No, no, no, no, no, no, no. EVERYBODY!

All the girls in all the other schools and . . . the boys. All the BOYS were there to see it!

All of them. The fancy-nancy boys from St. Francis Was A Sissy, the gravely Jesuit boys from Venerable Gonzago of the Dolors, the horny boys from St. Patrick of the Ecstasies. ALL, ALL were watching you. I wonder what they thought. I saw some in the shrubbery. Puking and pissing. Sickened by the score.

And all who didn't see the game . . . except the Dead . . . will read all about it in the papers! "Catholic Schoolgirls Clobbered in Playoffs by Protestant Twats." Something like that, I imagine.

"Our Lady of Exquisite Torments Trounced by Heretics!"

"Nun's Dream of Interscholastic Triumph Deep-Sixed by Own Fifth Graders!"

I wonder if His Holiness the Pope will read of our shame in English, Italian, Latin, or Poland? I'm only glad he wasn't here to see it. But of course your parents were. Those of you who have any. They're far from proud tonight. Except for your mummy, Margaret Ann! She passed out at the top of the Seventh just as you were being tagged out at First. She probably thinks we won! That's something to be said for drink!

And those of you who've lost your parents . . . Well! Maybe now we know why! *(Suddenly SHE addresses someone in audience.)*

HEY! MISSY! CLOSE UP THOSE LEGS. BE QUICK ABOUT IT!

I'VE GOT AN EYE ON YOU!

Oh, no, this is more than disgrace. It's . . . a breach of

faith! A thrashing, whipping, drubbing of every Catholic man, woman, and child.

"THOUGH ANGELS SWEET
THEIR BLESSED WATCH KEEP
OE'R PAPISTS FROM ON HIGH,
ALL INFIDELS AND JEWS IN HELL
DANCE JIGS WHEN CATHOLICS CRY!"

(Suddenly SHE addresses same person in audience SHE'd addressed before.)

HEY! WHAT'D I TELL YOU! CHOP, CHOP!
AND KEEP 'EM SHUT!

(SHE addresses someone else.)

YOURS TOO! WHAT ARE YOU GIGGLING AT?

(Pause.) CHOP, CHOP! Sluts.

And you, Cecelia Louise, our so-called Slugger! Wipe that smirk off your face. I suppose you're proud, are you, of your pathetic little FIVE homers? I wouldn't be, dear. Remember girls: Scripture says, "Pride goeth before a fall!" For everyone but you, dear, it's simple arithmetic, isn't it, class. In a game lost SEVEN to SIX, FIVE simply isn't enough! But God's displeasure with Cecelia Louise doesn't come as a surprise. He's already put His Mark of Cain on her face with all those awful pits. If you'd only put more energy into your swings and less in trying to get Mary Ellen to feel your biceps, perhaps you'd have given us our win. What good are your biceps now, Cecelia Louise? No one's wants to feel up the biceps of a loser! Not even lumpy little Mary Ellen, I should think. Anyway . . . I'VE ALREADY SPOKEN TO MOTHER SUPERIOR ABOUT YOU TWO! WE'VE GOT OUR EYES ON YOU!

Stop crying, Lucinda Lucanne! You're so much more unattractive when you cry. All your zits light up, like big red light balls on a Christmas tree! What WERE you doing in center field today? It certainly WASN'T out-fielding!

THE POP-UP YOU MISSED IN THE BOTTOM OF THE SEVENTH COULD'VE BEEN CAUGHT BY A QUAD-RIPLEGIC! If he wasn't smoking. And as for the sun in your eyes, even Mother Superior said, "What a load of Bull crap!"

If God'd wanted sun in someone's eyes He'd have socked it to those Protestant twats, not you! And certainly NOT at such a critical moment in the game. It wasn't the sun in your eyes, Lucinda Lucanne. It was DICK. Dick, Dick, Dick! Little Dickie what's-his-name. Little blond Dickie of St. Francis Was A Sissy! He's the only son you had in your eyes. I saw you! At game time. Giggling together! Laughing at his antics. Grinning like the little gorilla you resemble with those extralong arms and hands of yours. No lady's gloves but baseball gloves will ever hide those mitts of yours, dear!

Please remember that! And Peggy Sue! We mustn't forget our shortstop, class. Our Lady of Exquisite Torments has never had a shorter one than you, Peggy Sue. Or one who dropped more balls! I've always wondered why you girls call her "Piggy Sue" behind her back. Now I think I know! Oink, oink! Perhaps if you didn't still wet the bed, perhaps if you weren't up all night changing bed linen so your friends wouldn't find out, you'd feel better, dear. Sister Rose Margaret told me she helps you hide it from the class. But, hey! You're a team!

More Openness might've brought Victory today instead of Defeat! So tonight, when you wet your bed . . . Jump up! Turn on the lights! Oink! Wake up the team! Let THEM change you stinky sheets! And don't blame Sister Rosy for breaking her confidence with you. This may surprise you, but she and I are like THAT!

(SISTER violently slaps softball and bat together.)

She's putty in my hands. I forced her. To tell me. I mean. After your shoddy performance today, I bet you're glad your daddy died last year, aren't you, dear? You see, girls, in every so-called tragedy there's always a silver lining. What seems sad at first may later prove a blessing in disguise. Piggy Sue's daddy's drug-addicted death has always struck me that way. Now, you see, I was right!

He, at least, can't feel the shame the rest of us have to bear. But Piggy's not really the culprit today, is she class? That distinction goes to . . . you, Portia Colleen. Our STAR PITCHER . . . who threw the pitch that gave away the winning run! The Pitch the Protestant Bitch knocked outta the park. And THEN. If that weren't enough! Stood there on the pitcher's mound, and BLED!

> *Be the life of the party. Make us believe you know what you're doing. Even if you don't, make us believe you do. You come into the audition with as much confidence as you can and make us believe that that script was written for you.*
>
> **Charles Rosen, casting director,**
> **Casting by Rosen & Wojcik**

Chapter 11

COLD READING SCREENPLAYS AND TELEPLAYS

I want actors who know how to make a scene work, how to make themselves believable. Adding something to the scene that others didn't. Actors should make strong, definite choices and go with them. And, at the same time, they should be accessible to directions if they're given an adjustment.

**Lori Openden, senior vice president,
Talent and Casting, CW**

1. Review all the rules for cold reading plays. Most of the same rules apply to film and TV cold-reading auditions. The main difference between plays and screenplays is that movies are more visual. Much of the screenplay describes what the camera (and the audience) will be seeing at any moment. Allow the images to affect your work. The screenwriter will sometimes tell you what your character is seeing, feeling, and doing. How much of this you want to include in your audition is up to you. As always, you should make, strong, personal choices based what's going on in the story.

   • What is this scene about? What is the film about? If you don't have enough information from the sides to get a sense of what the movie is about, then just use your imagination.

- Try to discover the world that this film takes place in. Is it a comedy or a drama?

- Who is the character your playing? Once you get a take on him, figure out how you can identify with him. Two good questions to ask yourself after you read the script are: How am I like this character? How am I not like this character? These questions are a starting point that may help get you inside the piece quickly. However you can identify with the character will be helpful in your audition.

- Where is the character? A scene that takes place in a prison cell will play very differently than a scene at a party.

- What time of day or night does this scene take place? A scene that takes place at two in the afternoon will probably require a different energy than one that takes place at four in the morning.

- What does he want (the intention) and what is preventing him from getting it (objective)? Knowing (and playing) the intention and finding (and playing) the conflict is crucial to any scene.

- Try to get a sense of what your character feels in this scene. Do his emotions change as the scene progresses?

- What is the relationship between your character and the character(s) in the scene? Do your feelings change toward the other character as the scene progresses?

- If you have time, think about your character's background, his history.

- Always look at the page number of the scene that you're auditioning for. If it's early in the play, the relationship of the characters may not have been well developed yet. If the sides are from late in the play, you might assume that the characters have developed throughout the play. There is, of course, the chance that your character is meeting a new character in the play in a later scene (but it's not usually the case).

- Truth is truth is truth in acting. Your portrayal of the character, whether for stage, TV, or film, emanates from the same place inside you. The main difference between theater auditions and film auditions is the size of your performance.

2. Unless told to by the casting director, you shouldn't do your entire audition looking directly at the camera lens.

3. In film more than theater, reacting to what's happening and being said is most important. In the theater, we generally watch the person who's speaking. In film, quite often the edited scene focuses on the person listening and reacting.

4. Film and TV are much more intimate mediums: you don't have to spend as much energy as you would onstage. You're not playing to the back row of the theater here.

5. Much of what you communicate in TV and film is seen in your eyes. Again, if you're just doing your work, inhabiting the character, the camera will pick this up in your performance.

6. Generally there is less dialogue in screenplays than in plays. Screenplays are very visual; there's less need for talk. Again, all the more reason to focus on your reaction on what's being said.

7. Your posture on camera is very important. Don't slump in a chair or stand poorly unless you've made a specific character choice that this is how your character would sit or stand.

8. Your behavior will emanate from your thoughts and feelings. In film, your behavior, how your character (you) expresses himself, is of prime importance. We want to see a living breathing human being on that screen.

9. In an attempt to bring genuine life to the character in the scene, many screen directors encourage their actors to improvise at auditions, in rehearsals, or when actually shooting the scene. One bit of advice: if you haven't taken a good improvisation class, take one as soon as possible.

10. When you are auditioning for film and TV, be aware of how you're being framed by the camera. Generally, you're being framed from your chest up to the top of your head. If you move too much, you'll go out of frame.

11. The slate occurs after the casting direction says action. The slate is the way you identify yourself at the audition. The less you do, the better. I've seen actors make their slate too big, trying to impress the casting team by saying silly things or trying to impress them. Just look directly into the camera, have a genuine "nice to meet you" smile and say your name. Keep it simple.

12. The moment after the slate is "your" moment to prep yourself. Hopefully, you've been preparing in the waiting area when you read the script and have made specific choices. Now is your chance to express what you've decided to do. Allow yourself to shift from the business-friendly formality of the slate to the character you've decided to play. Give yourself the moment (a few seconds). Don't rush right into the scene.

13. Take your time and make sure your movements aren't too fast for the camera to pick up.
14. At the end of the read, stay in character until the casting director says cut! or thank you.

Sometimes actors are in character when they come into an audition. If I can pick that up, if I get that, I'll tell the director, "Let's just go into it and you can talk after." I like it when an actor tells me that he'd rather talk after if he's already in character. Although some directors like to chat first, if I see the actor's in character, I let them know we'll talk after. I always provide actors as readers so you always have somebody to read off of. At the audition, I'm looking for choices, for colors, for layers. I love actors who take chances, make choices that are interesting, and go for it. Also, you always look for the actor who didn't make the obvious choice. Humor, even in a scene that may not call for it, can add a lot. Humor can encapsulate a lot, and it really endears you to people.

Ronnie Yeskel, casting director

Chapter 12

ANALYSIS OF
COLD READING FILM SCENES

What follows is a film scene for you to practice your cold-reading skills. Many of the same rules apply to a cold reading of a screenplay as to a play. I realize that they are different mediums, but your role as an actor is still the same: to interpret, to make personal choices, and to go with your choices. Again, review the previous scenes and information about cold readings.

LIKE FAMILY

An original screenplay by Glenn Alterman

Credits roll over: Exterior rural road. Evening. Winter. It is snowing steadily. The darkness is lit only by the headlights and taillights of a car, which keep disappearing and appearing around curves, over hills.

A little closer, and we can see it is a late-model American four-door driving along curvy, snowy, hilly roads. We see the car from a distance, making its way around tight turns, skidding a bit as it does. Whoever's driving doesn't really know how to handle this snow, but isn't slowing down much.

We move in close to the fender of the car and notice that

the nameplate of the car is broken, and the clumps of metal letters swing loosely with the motion of the car. The car moves off, and the taillights recede into blackness.

The credits end as we fade in on: Interior country home den. Evening. Close up on a highball glass. A man's hand pours whiskey into the glass.

MALE VOICE: Soda?

ANOTHER MALE VOICE: *(Quickly, agitated.)* No, straight up.

FIRST MALE VOICE: Here ya go.

> *(We follow the glass as it's carried into a cozy den. Although the decor is comfortable and casual, the three people in it are tense and noticeably upset.*
>
> *The glass stops in front of the face of RON HENSCHEL. RON is in his late twenties. His handsome face is creased with stress and splattered with grease.*
>
> *As RON reaches for the glass, we notice that his clothes are torn and dirty.)*

RON: Thanks. S'like I said, s'all we talked about.

> *(RON turns to HELEN sitting on an easy chair across from him. She is in her early thirties. Her pretty face is etched with concern.)*

HELEN: Really?

RON: Whole ride up. Mind if I smoke?

> *(HAROLD, standing next to the couch, is in his early forties, serious. He has been listening with concern but . . .)*

HAROLD: *(Automatically.)* Not in the house.

RON: Oh, sure, sorry. *(To HELEN.)* So Mom was talkin' a mile a minute. Y'know how she does.

HELEN: Yeah.

RON: An' Pop, Pop couldn't get a word in edgewise, who

could? You know her, always answering her own questions. Y'know like "What'll he be like—Hope he's nice." "Think he's tall—bet he is." Like that. Ba-bop, ba-bop, and on an' on. Rattling away, the whole ride up. *(RON takes another slug from his drink.)*

HELEN: So they were looking forward . . .

RON: . . . Thrilled, all of us! We couldn't wait to get here! Mean it happened so fast with you two. Meeting in Mexico, falling in love, getting . . . This was definitely a big deal us comin' here to Monroe to meet . . . ? *(Trying again.)* To meet . . . ? *(To HAROLD.)* I'm sorry . . .

HAROLD: Harold.

RON: Harold! I'm sorry, man. Jesus, my mind's like . . . I forgot you're . . . I'm totally unravelled.

(HAROLD comfortingly pats him on the shoulder.)

HAROLD: That's OK, just relax.

HELEN: How far had you gotten?

RON: Just a few miles outta town. There was this road we were goin' up . . . This small . . . round an' round, corners and curves. But no lights. There were no lights there, anywhere.

HAROLD: Bryn Road, I bet.

RON: *(Accelerating as it unfolds.)* Yeah, Bryn Road, that's right. We took it to the top. Top of this, uh, hill or mountain, whatever it was. I'm not sure 'cause I was lookin' out the window, watchin' the snow fall, my mind like miles away, half listening to Mom yak, Pop tryin' to talk, the radio. But then I noticed the moon had gone behind a cloud. We'd just got to the top of this hill or whatever, an' I noticed it's pitch-black out; couldn't see a thing. An' maybe, maybe there was ice on the road, I dunno, but like all of a sudden, the car started to skid, slide down, the other side. An' Dad, well, the car was a rental, and maybe he didn't . . . All I know is we were goin' down, fast! *(Ron leans forward, on the edge of his seat.)* Sliding! Skidding! He kept turnin' the wheel, but no, nothing! Down! Goin' down in the dark, in the pitch-black! Faster! Spinning! OUT OF CONTROL! 'Til I think, think we hit a guardrail or . . . 'Cause I heard like a sound. Like a loud . . . ! Then we broke through, went over, down, kept falling. Falling! Felt like . . . All I could think was "Oh God, God, why now?! NO! WHY NOW!" Then crash! Glass. Things flying, everywhere!

   (Caught up in the horror, HELEN, cuts him off, touching his knee.)

HELEN: Did she scream?!

RON: *(Staring at her.)* Mom? No, wasn't time. Happened . . . Everything . . . ! Happened so fast! *(Collapsing back into the cushions.)* Then it like . . . it just . . . stopped. Quiet. Suddenly it was still. Very still, except for the horn. The damn horn was . . . wouldn't stop. Like one long . . . Beeping. Loud! Then I saw . . . In the front . . . Dad's head was . . . He . . . *(He stops himself, then looking away, softly.)* No . . . No one screamed.

HELEN: *(Softly.)* God.

HAROLD: You're lucky to be alive.

RON: Yeah.

   (They are all quiet for a moment. HAROLD comforts HELEN, his arm around her shoulders.)

HAROLD: You OK?

HELEN: Yeah.

HAROLD: Need another drink, Ron?

RON: *(Extending his glass.)* Please.

(HAROLD takes RON's glass, goes back to the bar.)

RON: *(Still upset, continuing.)* When the cops showed up, I was . . . Guess I didn't make any sense. Couldn't . . . They musta thought . . .

HELEN: *(Taking his hand, holding it.)* You were probably in shock.

RON: I guess. 'Cause I didn't know who I was, or where . . . ? Couldn't even remember why I was here in Monroe. Not even my name; let alone yours or this address. Then at the hospital, when I heard the cop say to the doc behind the desk, "D.O.A.," I actually thought he was talking 'bout me, yeah, tellin' them that I was de . . . I mean I was that out of it! Later on, in the waiting room, with the sheriff, things started coming back, slowly. I started to remember. Remembered where you guys lived, why we were in Monroe. Then they drove me out here, dropped me off. I asked them to let me come in alone so I could . . .

(HAROLD brings RON his drink.)

HELEN: Where'd they put them?

RON: Dad and Mom? The morgue. I told the sheriff we'd call 'em tomorrow to tell 'em what we wanted to do. *(To HAROLD, taking a gulp of his drink.)* Thanks. *(RON starts to take out his cigarettes again, realizes, then puts them back in his pocket.)* The doc said he was sure they never felt anything. "On impact! Instantly, both of . . ."

HELEN: Enough, please! *(HELEN gets up, goes to the window.)*

RON: I'm sorry. I just . . .

(The phone rings, HAROLD picks it up.)

HAROLD: Yeah. Hi. Listen, can I call you. . . ? . . . Again? All right, thanks, be right there. . . Yeah. *(He hangs up, goes to HELEN at the window.)* It's the restaurant, they're having trouble with the locks again.

HELEN: Again?

HAROLD: They can't leave. I have to go into town, help them close up.

HELEN: Now?

HAROLD: *(Apologetic, putting his arms around her.)* What can I . . . ? I have to, I'm sorry. Will you be OK?

HELEN: I'll be fine.

HAROLD: You sure?

HELEN: Yeah.

HAROLD: You, Ron?

RON: *(Holding his glass up.)* Sure.

HAROLD: I'll get my coat.

 (Harold walks out of the den. HELEN stares out the window, then slowly turns to RON. RON looks up at her.)

RON: *(Whispering.)* I wanna fuck you so bad.

HELEN: *(Turning back to the window, whispering.)* Are you crazy?

RON: God, I've missed you.

HELEN: Shut up, he can hear!

RON: *(Getting up.)* I just . . .

HELEN: Sit down! *(HELEN turns. RON stands there. Forcefully.)* Sit!

 (RON sits back down, reaches for his drink, still looking at her. HAROLD returns, putting on his coat.)

HAROLD: *(To HELEN.)* You need anything in town?

HELEN: No. How long will . . . ?

HAROLD: I just have to help them close out. Be twenty minutes, tops.

HELEN: Be careful.

HAROLD: I will. *(He kisses her.)* Be right back. *(He waves to RON as he leaves.)*

ANALYSIS OF LIKE FAMILY

Things to keep in mind when working on a cold-read audition for this movie:

1. From the beginning we are told that it's a cold, snowy night in a house in upstate New York. We discover there has been a fatal car accident. Notice the effect of this event on the three characters in the scene. Particularly notice the effect on the character that you're auditioning for.

2. Be sure to find a strong preparation for your character that you can use before you start your audition.

3. You want to play these characters as lifelike and natural as you can. They are having an intense discussion that you want to make as real as possible. Speak as yourself in the imaginary situation.

4. Notice the relationship of the three characters in the scene and how at a pivotal moment (the twist), the relationship between two of the characters changes radically. Decide what your character wants in the scene (intention). Does that change after the twist? One clue: Ron is *not* her brother.

5. What is your character feeling in the scene? Are the emotions he's showing his real feelings or is it an act?

6. You must decide if the accident really occurred and how you want to tell and react to the story about the accident. One tip: Don't show your cards if your character is (pos-

sibly) lying. Remember your first impression of the story in the scene as you originally read it. Be aware of how you reacted to the moment that the twist occurred. You want an audience to have that same reaction. You never want to play the end of the scene (the twist) at the beginning.

7. Decide how you want to play Ron's and Helen's new relationship after the moment of the twist. What new feelings enter the scene at that moment? How will you cover them up when Harold comes back into the room?

8. Ask yourself how you're like and not like the character you're playing.

9. Try to figure out what's at stake here and make sure your audition includes the urgency required in the scene.

10. Make strong, personal choices about your character and go for it!

What follows is a scene from a screenplay by Anastasia Traina to use as exercise material. Review the previous information on breaking down the scene. Don't forget to decide what the given circumstances are, to personalize the role that you're playing, to play the relationship of the characters, to decide what your character wants and is feeling, to make strong choices, and to have a good prebeat that will get you into the scene.

THE GLASS TANK

By Anastasia Traina

JACK ROBES—*thirties to early forties—is a scientist who was kicked out of MIT for drug use. He is now a stay-at-home dad of three. In this scene, Jack is visiting his old partner who went on to win a prestigious award for the work Jack did.*

The door opens to WALDO's private room in the asylum. The orderly starts to enter the room. JACK stops him.

JACK: I think I can handle it from here . . .
> *(JACK closes the door. He takes pause before he turns around. He turns to see WALDO now a small frail man with blue eyes the size of saucers. He is sitting at a blank desk as he stares into space and a little beyond. JACK steps closer.)*

JACK: Waldo?
> *(JACK notices oozing blisters on WALDO's lips and burn marks on the side of WALDO's temples. WALDO meets JACK's gaze. A faint light starts to spark in WALDO's eyes, he looks away. Moments pass in silence.)*

WALDO: You shouldn't have come here . . .

JACK: I—

WALDO: You know how goddamn narcissistic I can be . . .

JACK: Well, now that you mention it I do remember you being a bit of a prick—

WALDO: *(Shaking his head.)* Go ahead Jack . . . attack a man while he's sitting down wearing hospital issue—
> *(JACK laughs as he gets up and hugs WALDO.)*

JACK: It's good to see you old man.
> *(WALDO pushes him away.)*

WALDO: *(Pushing JACK away.)* Watch it! I just had the paper pressed—

JACK: I'm so glad you are all right, I thought, I thought—

WALDO: Even madmen have their good days.

JACK: You seem all right—

WALDO: Define all right . . .
> *(JACK bows his head.)*

WALDO: I'm glad you came.

> *(JACK looks up.)*

WALDO: I've been wanting to say something—

JACK: There's no need—

WALDO: *(Slamming his hand on the table.)* Oh for Christ-sakes— You come here to gloat where my greed has led me?

JACK: No Waldo— This was a mistake, I'm sorry. *(JACK gets up and turns away to leave.)*

WALDO: You were always the better man . . .

> *(JACK starts walking out. JACK turns back to WALDO.)*

JACK: Waldo? I came hear to ask—to talk to you about certain things—Things that have been happening to me . . .

> *(JACK stares at the ceiling. WALDO looks down at his slippers.)*

JACK: I'm feeling outside of things—things from my—

WALDO: Listen to me! I have turned my attention elsewhere, I now invest my thoughts in shoes.

JACK: Don't fuck around, Waldo.

> *(WALDO leans into JACK.)*

WALDO: Listen to me, this is very important. Tonight you must leave your shoes at the bedroom door so that one shoe is coming into the room and the other is going out of the room. Promise me. Promise me! *(WALDO looks down to his slippers again and then slowly slips them off.)*

JACK: I promise.

> *(WALDO wiggles his toes in the air.)*

WALDO: Good. Very good. No, I was wrong . . . I was wrong because . . . it is not really the shoes that are important here, but . . . feet. Because I have turned my attention to feet. Feet are very important. They carry a great weight. They hold one erect. And most important of all . . . they can take you where you want to go.

(WALDO has drifted far out to sea. JACK searches for his friend. He seems to have disappeared. JACK's beeper buzzes. He checks the number.)

JACK: Waldo, I'm going to go now . . . *(JACK kisses WALDO's forehead and heads for the door.)*

WALDO: *(Mumbles to himself.)* Quis custodiet ipsos custodes?

(JACK turns back to WALDO.)

WALDO: Quis custodiet ipsos custodes?

JACK: Waldo?

(WALDO turns toward JACK.)

JACK: . . . Who watches the watchman?

(WALDO turns away. JACK buzzes the red button. The door opens. JACK looks back to WALDO one last time and then leaves.)

WALDO: *(Laughing.)* You do.

(The door slams shut.)

Chapter 13

INTERVIEWS WITH CASTING DIRECTORS OF PLAYS, SCREENPLAYS, AND TELEPLAYS

Peter Golden (PG), executive vice president, Talent and Casting, CBS

Stuart Howard (SH), Stuart Howard Associates, Ltd.

Scott Wojcik (SW), senior casting director, Casting by Rosen & Wojcik

Harriet Bass (HB), Harriet Bass Casting

Stephanie Laffin (SL), casting director, *House*

1. What things do you think actors should be looking for when reading the sides of a script for the first time?

PG: Because, by their very nature, cold readings are far from finished performances, you [actors/actresses] should attempt to present a point of view on a character that represents your quick take on that character, your unique essence. Look for specifics in the dialogue that you can make your own.

SH: Well, to be honest, an actor shouldn't only have looked at the sides for a play. Why hasn't he read the entire script? I can only think of a few instances in the past ten years when we have cast a play when it has not been available for an actor to read. There are too many actors who simply read at their audition. What does this tell the casting director? Well, in the best of all possible worlds, it does tell us you are intelligent and can make sense of the English language. In a play of Shakespeare's, it, hopefully, tells us that you can handle poetry, but it doesn't tell us who you are. It doesn't tell us what you might bring to the role should you be cast. Make choices.

SW: The initial read-through should give the actor a sense of the relationships within the scene and provide clues as to how to create an arc in the action so that clear and strong choices can be made to best demonstrate the actor's viability for the role.

HB: I think an actor should quickly scan new sides to get an idea of what has to happen in the scene. They should look for clues to understanding their relationship with the other characters, and then plan the actions that will help them to achieve their "wants" in the scene.

SL: I always think that it's the actor's responsibility to figure out who the person in the sides is. Specifically, if the character is a doctor, what type of doctor is he and what kind of hospital does he work in. If there are certain terms that the actor is unfamiliar with (legal terms, medical diagnosis), the actor should do the research to find out exactly what the words mean. Also, the actor should look for clues regarding the character relationships within the sides. Are the characters friends, adversaries, or romantically involved?

2. An actor reads for you, and you realize that he is better suited for another character in the piece. You give him the sides for the new character and tell him to go out

and take a look at it and come back in a few minutes (thus a cold read). What do you expect from him in the new audition when he returns?

PG: If I've given you sides for a new character, it means I've seen something in you that feels more appropriate for the new character. Again, as above, find the essence of what the character and you have in common and present that point of view.

SH: I expect that the actor will have read the entire script and, therefore, will know who the new character is, what this character wants, and how he is going to get it. Therefore, the actor can make interesting choices when reading the new role. I don't know about other casting directors, but when we give an actor the script to look at for a new role, we don't say, "And be ready in five minutes." We say, "Tell us when you'll be ready to read." A variation on this actually just happened. We were casting Shakespeare's *Titus Andronicus,* and one woman was auditioning for the major role of Tamara. Her agent had only downloaded one scene for her to audition with but actually three scenes had been provided online. After she read the first scene, I gave her the additional scenes and asked when she might be ready. She said, "Just give me a few minutes. I know the play. I've read it several times and really prepared for this audition. So as soon as I know which scenes they are, I can come right in."

SW: Same answer as for question 1.

HB: I would expect the actor to understand the difference between the two characters that he or she has now read for and show me something to indicate that difference. I would also expect the actor to try to understand what it is about him or her that made me change my mind in the first place, and so allow the actor's natural strengths and qualities to aid them through the new scene. An actor should also try, within the time allowed, to do as much scene study work as is possible, that is picking out beats and transitions, deciding on actions and motivations, and establishing relationships with the other characters. But, when all is said and done, the actor should know that we do understand that this is a cold reading and much of the homework that is expected to be done in any other audition situation is forgiven a bit here.

SL: Well, if we're asking the actor to come back in the room, we've clearly seen something we like. So, while we're not expecting the actor to be off-book or well memorized, we're expecting that he at least make a distinct choice regarding the character.

3. Any advice on cold readings that you feel may be helpful for actors auditioning for you?

PG: Yes! Listen to the person reading with you. One of the biggest mistakes actors make in auditions is *not* listening to their scene partner's dialogue. Listen, listen, listen!

SH: It is very hard for an actor *not* to become hysterically deaf, dumb, and blind during a regular audition for which he has planned and and prepared. It is even harder to be handed a new role to prepare in a matter of minutes or, at best, hours. What do I mean by "hysterically deaf, dumb, and blind"? It would be the inability of an actor to switch gears immediately, to listen and to hear what a director wants the actor to do, and to execute it as well as he possibly can. Don't make excuses for having a short period of time to prepare: everyone behind the table knows exactly what kind of time limit you had. Excuses of any kind don't really sit well with directors unless they are excuses that really have meaning. For example, very recently we were casting a play for which an actor came in and gave a fine reading. The director asked him to come back in a few days—our final day of auditions before the director went home to Australia. He read again very well, but this time the director realized that he should be reading a different role. She asked him to look at the role and come back in about a half hour. He smiled and said he'd do it. He came back and made a total mess of the text. He stumbled over words again and again and didn't really make sense. What the actor never told us, which we learned from his agent the following day, was that he is dyslexic and simply needed more time to prepare. Why couldn't he have let us know? This certainly is one "excuse" that everyone in the room would have understood and honored.

SW: Cold reading is a skill, and an actor should know how good he is at it and take steps to get better if he can't show his best work in a cold reading.

HB: An actor should do as much prep work in a cold reading that time will allow and then trust the choices that he or she has made. The more honest and simple an audition is at this stage of the game, the better it will be.

SL: Make a choice and show us what's great about *you*. We're not expecting perfection; we just want to see why you are best suited for a role.

4. Specifically what do you expect from an actor at your auditions?

PG: I expect you to show me something, based on your interpretation of the role, that makes you uniquely able to play the character—something surprising about the character, something that wasn't on the page but that defines the character and makes the character a more fully realized individual.

SH: At *every* audition, I expect a sense of what it means to be a professional: have a photo and résumé (I mean, can one imagine a stockbroker or a teacher or a salesman going to a job interview without a résumé?), the sides for the audition, and good, strong preparation.

SW: Preparation, professionalism, and politeness mixed with strong choices and a relaxed disposition.

HB: An actor should come to every audition with his or her homework done. I expect professionalism and preparedness.

SL: Same answer as for question 3.

5. What do you feel are the biggest mistakes actors make at auditions?

PG: Even in cold readings, you must be completely present in each moment. You can not just be waiting for your cue to start speaking.

SH: Trying to guess what the people behind the desk want. It's a no-win situation. One cannot guess mainly because oftentimes the director does not even know what he wants until it is presented to him by the actor.

SW: Making choices outside the boundaries established by the sides; not enough preparation; not listening to the director or casting director when adjustments are offered.

HB: I think oftentimes actors try too hard, and the audition can become unnatural, pushed, or forced. I also think an actor can get so caught up in his own lines that that he may forget to listen. It is essential for us to see the actor relate to the reader by listening and reacting. What is important for an actor to remember is that the people sitting on the other side of the table want him to be good. They want him to be "the one." Remember, the better you look, the better we look.

SL: That they are familiar with the material that they've been given and that they make a choice and have an opinion about that material.

6. **If you had one piece of advice to offer actors regarding auditioning what would it be?**

PG: Listen, listen, listen. Even if you don't feel that you're physically right for a role, or if you feel that you're too young or too old, if you can find an organic connection, you may be able to change the way we are thinking about the role. But to accomplish that, you've got to appear to be hearing and saying the words in the scene for the first time—as in life. And to do that, you have to be listening.

SH: Be yourself; be confident without being arrogant; and please, never audition for a role you are not available to take.

SW: Don't need it too badly and keep each audition in perspective so the task will not intimidate you.

HB: Make clear choices and be real, honest, and even simple in those choices.

SL: An audition is a job interview, and it should be treated as a professional situation. Don't come in unprepared and say, as you walk into the room, "Well, I just got the material last night."

Chapter 14

50 THINGS YOU NEED TO KNOW ABOUT COLD READING TV COMMERCIALS

Before you even walk in the room to audition, you should read the instructions that are posted. I can't tell you how many actors don't. Ask questions if you need to. To be ignorant is not smart: The old saying, the only stupid question is the one you didn't ask.

I like it when actors enjoy my waiting area and are social; however, you shouldn't be too social, not at the expense of the audition. Look at the material and know what you're going to do when you walk in the audition room. It makes me nuts when someone walks in and says, "Oh gee, I didn't have a chance to look at the material."

Specifically, I look for enthusiasm, someone who listens, who wants to be there, who is going to try to give me what I want, who will work hard for me. If I see they're working hard to give me what I want, I'll work real hard for them. They'll get the best out of me, what I have to offer.

Donna DeSeta, casting director,
Donna DeSeta Casting

1. Most commercials are cold-reading auditions. You don't get the script in advance. You must be prepared to read the script and make quick, personal choices.

2. Try to dress appropriately for the commercial. TV commercials are very visual. If you're reading for a high-power executive, you should dress accordingly. That being said, if you're reading for a character that normally wears a uniform (police officer, nurse), you don't need to wear a specific costume, just suggest the type of clothing that the character would wear.

3. Always arrive early—at least fifteen minutes to a half hour before your actual audition time.

4. Don't chat with the other actors in the waiting area; this is not a time to socialize.

5. If there are any instructions outside the audition room, read them.

6. If there is a storyboard outside the audition room, study it and see what they're trying to tell you. (The storyboard is a frame-by-frame drawing of what the ad agency wants the commercial to look like.)

7. Try to get a sense of what the ad agency is doing to sell its product in this particular spot.

8. Get a feel for the mood and style of the piece. Is it a silly romp about candy or toys, or a serious commercial on why you should stop smoking?

9. Remember, the ad agency needs you, your personality, to sell its product. The more of "you" you can add to the read, the better.

10. Break down the copy in the script into playable beats.

11. Obviously, you must be aware of what the product is, what it is they're selling in this commercial.

12. Figure out what the selling points are in the commercial:

   - What makes this product special? How is it different from similar products?

   - Why can't people live without it?

   - How has this product changed or will change your life or other people's lives?

13. See where your character fits into the story of the commercial. He may need help or be the one suggesting that this product may be helpful to him. Most commercials are about a problem that the character is having, and the product resolves that problem.

15. When you are given your mark, make sure you stay there. Some actors wander out of frame.

16. Make sure you know where you are in the commercial. Your behavior (and read) will be different if you're in a singles bar or if you're in a supermarket. If it's not clearly indicated in the copy, use your imagination and decide where it takes place.

17. Be sure you're clear about the relationship with the other character in the commercial. Is she your daughter? Your wife? How do you get along with the other character in the commercial?

18. Make sure you're clear what your character wants in the commercial. It may be only thirty or sixty seconds, but what you want or need must be clear.

19. Always be sure you know how to pronounce all the words in the commercial, especially if there is any medical terminology.

20. Make sure you know exactly how to pronounce the name of the product! Nothing annoys ad agencies more than the frequent mispronunciation of their product.

21. Commercials are generally light-hearted. Try not to get too intense or dramatic during the audition.

22. If there is the potential for you to express different emotions, find them and play them. Be honest with what the copy is saying to express these emotions; don't overemote just for effect.

23. The hard sell in commercials is out. Generally, the current trend in commercials is to have relaxed, real people. There was a commercial years ago that spoofed the hard-sell approach. The product had a manic spokesman—Craazzy Eddie—screaming at you. It was funny and over the top. In today's marketplace, spokesmen (and women) should create an air of calm authority and confidence and yet be someone who is friendly and accessible.

24. Before you enter the room, think about what you want to achieve in the audition. Seeing yourself as confident, positive, and open is very helpful at all auditions, but especially at commercial auditions.

25. If you haven't had enough time to work on the script, and there are people ahead of you, let them go in first (if possible). You want to make sure that you're totally prepared before you enter that room. But if you've been paired up with another person for your audition, this won't be possible.

26. Enter the room with a cheerful, sincere smile. Make eye contact, and have lots of good energy.

27. If there are any instructions, listen to them. I realize that you may be nervous, but try to hear what the casting director is telling you. He is your lifeline between you and the client and the commercial. He may say something that isn't what you had in mind about the material. Quickly make the adjustment in your mind.

28. Be aware of your relationship to the target audience if you're talking directly to the camera.

29. If you're talking directly to the camera, you want to create the illusion that you're talking to either a good friend or a neighbor. Or perhaps you're talking to your son, daughter, or mother, depending on what's called for.

30. Look at the cue card next to the camera. The cue card contains the copy that was in the script you were working on in the waiting area. Notice if there are any changes in the copy.

31. Don't become overly concerned about shifting your gaze back and forth from the cue card to the camera. It may feel awkward, but it won't read that way when they watch the playback.

32. If you really have a question about the commercial copy, be sure to ask it. That's not saying you should ask unnecessary questions just because you're nervous and want to connect with the casting director. Be professional.

33. If, because you forgot your glasses, you cannot read the cue card, ask the casting director to move it closer so that you can read it. Don't blow an audition because you have to strain to read the cue card.

34. Smile during the slate. Some actors come across as too serious or even angry when they slate. The slate is the moment when you get to show your warmth and likability. In that brief moment, you are letting them know you're a nice person who would be fun to work with if you got the job.

35. You need to clearly say your name and agency (if asked for). Don't mumble. It's better to say "My name is Glenn Alterman. I'm repped by Innovative Artists," than to say the more abrupt, "Glenn Alterman, Innovative." In the

first slate, you have an opportunity to show a bit more of your personality.

36. If you're slating with another person, take a full second before beginning your slate.

37. Don't slate in character. Just be yourself and slate as a friendly, positive you. Some casting directors consider the slate to be one of the most important parts of the commercial audition. In that moment, the ad agency gets a sense of who you are.

38. After you slate, allow a few seconds before you start the commercial. It gives the client a moment to comment on your slate, and it also gives you a moment to get into the material and give a good audition.

39. If you're auditioning for a spokesperson, express some of your natural warmth. Some actors think spokesperson means cold and detached—not usually.

40. It's helpful to paraphrase when rehearsing the copy. Put the commercial copy into your own words so that you can better identify with what you're saying during the actual audition. But try not to add your own words to the copy at the actual audition.

41. If the commercial audition is a scene with another actor, listen and react to what he is saying. Even if you feel that he is not doing a good job, you must react to what his character is saying. Never let the other actor's bad performance at an audition bring down yours. The casting director will know that the other actor didn't do a good job and that you did.

42. If you fumble over a word or two, don't stop or react to your error. Don't mention it to the casting director after you tape. If the auditors want you to do it again, they'll

ask you. They're aware that this is a cold reading not a final performance.

43. If the scene is with another actor, you'll want to stand relatively close to the other actor. During the playback, you won't look that close. That being said, don't get uncomfortably close.

44. You are allowed to touch the other actor, but don't go overboard. A gentle kiss on the cheek if called for in the copy is allowed.

45. You should never direct the other actor in the commercial. If you have a chance to read with him before the actual audition, let him do his thing and you do yours.

46. Generally, it's advised not to memorize the copy at a commercial, especially if there is a lot of copy or it's a complicated scene. You may end up spending some of your audition time trying to remember what your next line is.

47. It's a good idea to memorize the first and last lines of the copy so that you can be looking directly at the camera at crucial times of the audition.

48. Look for the tagline. Usually the tagline is at the end of the commercial, but occasionally it will be at the beginning of the spot as well. The tagline sums up the main message of the commercial. It's usually the last thing the viewer will hear. You want to make a very clear and positive choice about how to play the tagline.

49. If you're given an adjustment after your read, make a good effort to give them what they ask for.

50. If you don't exactly understand what they're asking for in an adjustment, ask them to clarify. If you disagree with the adjustment they've requested, keep it to yourself. This is no time for a discussion. Just try to give them what they ask for to the best of your ability.

Commercial auditions are almost exclusively cold readings. In all my years as a commercial performer, I don't think I have ever received copy in advance. Being able to quickly analyze the copy and execute it specifically is a must for the successful commercial actor.

Because commercials are so compressed—usually no more than twenty-eight seconds of copy and often less—choices need to be very specific. Be aware of the stereotype they are seeking—young mommy, teacher, angry boss—because commercials deal in types. But make sure that your choices are not clichés. They are looking for your young mommy, not the generic one. Don't leave your personality out in the hallway. It is what makes you distinct from everyone else. Same goes for your sense of humor—it is uniquely you.

Use your acting skills. Commercials work because you, as the actor, make the scene happen. The selling is embedded (hopefully), and you do not sell. Make sure that you have a very clear, high-stakes need/intention/task. What do I want and how do I feel about it?—two very important questions you must answer as specifically as possible.

Commercials tend to be personal—you rarely talk to more than one person if you are addressing the camera. They usually feel relaxed, but your internal work must be (again) very specific and high stakes. This can be confusing for actors. They can get lulled by the conversational tone and forget to load in the important underpinnings of need and stakes.

Know what the relationship is and make it personal. If you are talking to a friend, choose a real friend and one who matters to you. Don't be afraid to substitute, but keep it in the same ballpark. If you are smelling lemon-scented laundry detergent and you hate lemon, make it your favorite smell. All they are looking for is your honest reaction to it.

While making clear actable choices is key, you must also be adept at changing those choices. They may direct you to try something different after the first take. Be ready to make the switch and commit to the new choice totally. Don't get trapped into holding onto the first idea you came in with.

And above all, fall in love with auditioning. Because you will do much more of that than anything else, and it is the door to the job.

Roberta Reardon, commercial acting coach, actress

Chapter 15

COLD READING VOICE-OVERS

Because I personally know very little about voice-over cold readings, I asked two professional voice-over instructors—David Zema (www.davidzema.com) and Steve Harris (TheArtofVoice@aol.com)—for their expert opinions about what it takes to give a good voice-over audition.

Voice-over performers encounter cold readings at auditions and jobs more often than other actors. Cold readings for voice-over performers are a regular day-to-day experience. On the same day, they may encounter a dramatic recorded novel, a jargon-filled industrial, an animation script, or a comedic commercial.

12 TIPS FOR COLD READING VOICE-OVERS
By David Zema (voice-over performer, producer, director, and coach)

To deliver excellent cold readings, the voice actor must be completely prepared for a reading before ever auditioning for the job. How is that possible? To help, I have a list of twelve tips voice actors can use to prepare for cold readings in advance. The letters that spell "cold readings" start each tip to make them easier to remember.

C is for Create a Character. To avoid sounding like a local announcer reading a spot, bring your characters with you.

Become the person speaking and talk as he or she would in the situation being presented. Learn to make what I call "AdSpeak" conversational. Working with a coach can help you develop a natural delivery of the most awkward writing.

O is for Original. Be yourself and bring something personal to the reading. This adds believability to your read and makes it stand out from the crowd.

L is for Live. Be in the moment of each situation; react to what you are talking about and stay involved with the message.

D is for Dynamic and Direction. Look for transitions, changes of emotion, and points to move the story along or bring out drama or comedy. Let the words be your director.

R is for Ready and Reading Skills. Warm up your voice and practice reading aloud daily to develop excellent reading skills. You will be more comfortable with difficult copy with better reading skills.

E is for Energy. Keep moving. Use gestures and facial expressions to bring energy and involvement to the reading.

A is for Awareness. Stay focused on what is happening in the story to avoid droning on out loud. Remember you are not actually reading aloud. Instead, you are speaking spontaneously. Become an expert who is telling the story to the most interested listener. Your keen awareness makes your performance compelling to listen to.

D is for Daring. Take risks. Add small filler words and expressions. Don't rewrite the copy, but it's OK to interject an occasional appropriate ad lib. It can help you book the job.

I is for Identification. Identify the following: Who is speaking? Who is listening? What are the main points to bring out? How does the speaker want the listener to feel about what is being said? Also, identify with the listener on a one-on-one level.

N is for Nuances. A picture may be worth a thousand words, but the voice adds personality and character, tone, emotions, importance, and all the specific communication that make the words meaningful.

G is for Go for It! Speak with confidence. Commit to your choices!

S is for Stay in Shape. Voice-over styles and trends for commercials change constantly. So stay on top of those trends. New media are also adding new styles for websites, podcasts, cell phones, and other new forms. Industrials, animation, and narration for books may not change as frequently, but the specific performance styles and characters needed must be mastered. Practice daily and work with a coach to keep up with the needs of the field.

COLD READING FOR VOICE-OVERS
By Steve Harris (commercial voice-over talent instructor)

A seasoned performer can look at script, mark the script, and then execute a very competitive reading. Voice-over or on-camera performers usually see the text for the very first time at the casting session and for the most part spend a few minutes looking over the script and make some important choices while waiting to be called in to read. Strong reading instincts are important for the performer who wants to work. Performers who practice reading daily are often most agile, take very good directions, and execute better cold-reading performances. Those not practicing such a daily regimen can become very rusty and mechanical. Casting professionals can hear the difference between a seasoned warmed-up performer and an out-of-shape one. I'm a strong believer in practicing all reading performances into a recording device and then listening back. The listening process helps train the ears and develop a strong sense of self-awareness during performance.

Once directed to make adjustments, such as a vocal style, delivery, or attitude, the performer must be able to execute those adjustments instantly.

A big problem for the casting professional or spot producer is auditioning new performers who cannot adjust their performance for a second take at the audition. This is a clear indication to the casting director of a performance limitation.

Talented, well-skilled cold readers often go to an audition with a range of vocal tones, styles, and attitudes and may tap into any one of their abilities instantly. Talented cold readers also offer a wider range of vocal range, attitudes, and personality, thereby making their performance abilities appealing to a wider range of projects and purposes.

Chapter 16

INTERVIEWS WITH CASTING DIRECTORS OF TV COMMERCIALS

*I look for creativity and choices. Be the life of the party.
Make us believe you know what you're doing. Even if you
don't, make us believe you do. You come into the audition
with as much confidence as you can and make us believe
that that script was written for you.*

**Charles Rosen, casting director,
Casting by Rosen & Wojcik**

Tisha Ioli (TI), casting director, Donald Case Casting, New York
Donna Grossman (DG), casting director, Donna Grossman Casting,
 New York
Erica Palgon (EP), casting director, Liz Lewis Casting Partners,
 New York
Elsie Stark (ES), casting director, Stark Naked Productions,
 New York

1. What things should an actor look for when reading commercial copy for the first time?

TI: An actor should try and make the copy as personal as
 possible, and by that I mean, let your personality show.
 You have to understand that we are probably seeing

somewhere between twenty-five to sixty people for each role, depending on the client's requirements, and with that kind of volume, the performances that will stand out from the rest will come from actors who manage to make the copy their own. The majority of actors we audition read the copy the exact same way. I think a smart actor can use that information to his advantage by choosing to find a way to vary a piece of copy slightly, in a way that feels natural to him, and without going over the top.

DG: When reading commercial copy for the first time, an actor should determine the following:
- Who is the character that I am portraying?
- What is it I am trying to say?
- Who am I speaking to?
- How can I make this my own?

EP: The first and most important thing to know when you arrive at an audition is to find out what role you are reading for. Many times, actors come into the studio and realize they have looked at the wrong role. Usually, you only have a short time to look at the copy, so if you are not sure, *ask*. Also, read everything: the dialogue *and* the stage directions. It is there for a reason. Try practicing putting the lines in your own words to make the tone come through more natural and comfortable. Then rehearse it with the actual lines. Another helpful tool to look for when you arrive at the audition is the storyboard. A storyboard shows, shot by shot, what is going on in the commercial. Some advertisements are strictly visual, and there is no copy to prepare. In this case, most casting directors will have a description of the spot available to look at. Again, read everything!

ES: The actor should look at the entire picture of the story not just what he or she is saying or doing. Read what the announcer is saying because it will give you ideas about the point of view of the spot. If anything is unclear, be ready to asked the casting director your question.

2. What kinds of things do you expect from an actor at your auditions?

TI: I think what we expect from actors is the same thing that is expected from anyone interviewing for a job in an office setting. Be professional. Show up on time. Be prepared (by that I mean, have a pen with you and bring a headshot and résumé just in case we ask for one). Take the time to look over the script and any notes that we put out for you, and ask questions if something is unclear. Other things like being polite, respecting the space that you are auditioning in, and keeping down the noise in the waiting room fall under the commonsense category.

DG: I think it is a real gift to be able to listen and take direction. An actor that can listen, take direction, and give us a variety of reads if we need them is a true find. At my auditions, I expect actors to come prepared. By prepared, I mean arrive at the audition at least fifteen minutes before their confirmed appointment so that they can review the copy, mark it where necessary, and become comfortable with it. I also expect them to come with a current picture and résumé and dressed appropriately for the character they are portraying. For example, if an actor is auditioning for a role as a businessperson, I expect him to be dressed as such; to arrive in cargo shorts and a T-shirt at a business audition shows a lack of respect for the casting director and for the industry.

EP: I expect actors to treat acting like a job. Be prepared. No excuses. You should always have a picture and résumé with you, even if you haven't been asked to bring one.

Casting directors are always working on multiple projects, and it is to your advantage to have several with you at all times. And no blaming. Even if you have an agent, you must take responsibility for your own career. Get as much information as possible. Wardrobe for an audition is also very important, and if the agent or casting director does not tell you what you should wear, ask them. The type of role will also help you to determine your wardrobe. I expect actors to know when the commercial shoots or records prior to coming to the audition. Is there travel involved? If you are not available for the project, you should not be auditioning. In addition, I expect actors to be on time for their auditions. Lateness is very unprofessional. You should arrive at the time that you are scheduled for. There are reasons why casting directors schedule auditions a certain way. If you were constantly late for a "normal" job, it would not be tolerated. The same should be applied to acting. Lastly, actors should act professionally toward everyone; this means fellow actors, casting directors, interns, assistants—whoever. There is no excuse for bad behavior no matter how talented you are. Use your head, don't act helpless, and be proactive.

ES: I expect professionalism. I expect them to be on time, use the time in the waiting room wisely by going over the scripts and/or storyboards, have their picture and résumé ready, and be up to the challenge in competing against their fellow performers.

3. What are the biggest mistakes actors make at commercial auditions?

TI: Comments I seem to hear myself saying often are, "Try it again, but sell it. Don't push it. Just tell me about it." If an actor listens to his voice while reading the copy and it doesn't sound like the way he talks when he is at home, he's probably not doing it right. The copy should always sound as natural as possible and remind an actor of the way he would convey this information to a friend or neighbor. Commercials have changed over the years. The hard sell is out. What's in and very popular is the regular person on the street who just happens to believe in the product. Other mistakes: Not taking the time to rehearse if you are given the opportunity, trying to memorize the copy (which always trips you up), and keeping your hands in your pockets or frozen by your side. It is much better to use your whole body. Let your hands move if they want to. A relaxed body will read well on camera. Finally, don't stop in the middle of your audition and say, "Can I do that again?" Be professional. Carry on, get through it, and let us decide whether or not we feel the need to erase and re-record.

DG: I believe all actors have something to offer, so it's difficult for me to pinpoint mistakes. For me, it's all about mutual respect. If an actor arrives on time (not hours early or hours late), signs in, studies his copy, and walks into my studio prepared and with an open mind, it's all good. I like to begin an audition with having the actor do his first reading without my direction; this gives me a sense of how he interpreted the material. From that point on, it's all about listening. If a casting director is taking the time to give an actor notes on his or her reading, that actor should listen carefully and try his or her best to make any adjustments necessary. I suppose that would be the biggest mistake an actor could make—not listening. That's critical. Not only does failure to listen result in a poor audition, it also confirms a lack of respect for the casting director.

EP: Most common mistakes actors make are: Signing in at the wrong audition. Showing up late and expecting to be seen. Crashing auditions—sneaking into auditions you don't have an appointment for. Spacing out, not focusing, and not listening to the direction from the casting director or director. Socializing with friends instead of working on the copy. Another big mistake actors make when reading copy is trying too hard to sell the product. We don't want to see the "selly" actor. The key is to be as real and natural as possible.

ES: Not being prepared and apologizing right after a take. You need to be confident from the minute you walk in to the minute you leave. If you prepared and you did your best, then you have nothing to apologize for.

4. If you had one piece of advice to offer actors regarding commercial auditions, what would it be?

TI: There are so many practical tips I could give an actor, but if I can only choose one that falls under the category of advice, I would have to say, get in there and do your best and then forget about it. Leave the audition without regret. Know in your heart that you did your best, and if you don't feel as if you did your best, know that there will always be a next time. Sometimes it's just a look. No matter how good you are or how much you aced the audition and deserve the commercial, if we are matching people to be part of a family and you don't look enough like someone who fits that "family," the actor with a lot less talent, but the right look will get the job. I see it all the time.

DG: Don't be fearful and intimidated by a casting director. It's counterproductive. As casting directors, our job is to direct the actors and get their best possible audition on tape so that they can get work. If the audition is not good, we have not done our job. Have an open mind to what a casting director offers you, take any critique as constructive criticism, and use it to your benefit.

EP: Remember, casting directors want you to do well. We are not out there to sabotage your audition. We want you to get the job. Listen to what we are telling you. Pay attention and follow the direction the best way you can. Casting directors, advertising agencies, and directors are looking for you to be creative and show them your take on the character. Take an improv class to open up that creativity, observe people, and watch current TV commercials.

ES: Respect the art form that commercials are. Telling a story within sixty seconds or less that gets people's attention and is memorable is tough. Some actors think that commercials are fluff or don't think that it merits that same respect as a film or a theatrical play. That is the worst mistake. I have seem some of the finest actors stumble and bumble because they didn't take it seriously. Knowing your craft is what it's all about. If you want to be a serious actor, then you need to have the talent and the flexibility to act in all the mediums of the industry.

Do not come in unprepared. Come to the audition on time. Don't talk or socialize; get prepared. Sit and read your copy and get to know it, so when you come in you can have an exchange with the casting director and be free enough to be creative. I specifically look for the look, the way actors carry themselves. Sometimes I don't know anything until the actor opens his mouth. I generally am looking for someone who is comfortable on camera, who knows what he's doing. The most important thing actors needs to know is that the casting director needs them as much as they need us.

Liz Lewis, casting director, Liz Lewis Casting Partners

*I want actors to be prepared; to know that they under-
stand commercials and the medium right off the bat. I
want an actor who does all the work and is now ready to
come into the audition room and be available to take direction. I look for an actor who isn't muddled by what he's
thinking as opposed to what he should be listening to. Be
professional.*

Toni Roberts, commercial casting director

*There are a couple of things to always keep in mind about
commercials and reading commercial copy:*

*1. Actors don't star in commercials: Products star in
commercials.*

2. It's not brain surgery.

*3. Reading cold is probably the best way to do it. That's why
casting directors don't give you the copy ahead of time.*

Let's take them one at a time. Commercials are about
selling something, not about acting. They almost always
involve people (i.e., you, the actor) feeling good, sexy, attractive, positive, healthy, secure, rich, beautiful, or otherwise happy because you had the good fortune to use—
THE PRODUCT. What that means is that you have to be
honest, real, convincing, and natural when you deliver the
copy. It also means that unless you're playing an animated
string bean or a dancing mop (when you have a bit of li-
cense to go over the top and maybe use a funny voice),
you should be as real as possible.

Commercial copy is short, sweet, to the point, and
real. The best thing to do is watch television or listen to
the radio. You'll hear immediately what they're looking
for. Often, it's an intimate, natural read: as if you're telling

your best friend some great news in a completely comfortable setting. ("Continental. Work hard. Fly right." "Olive Garden. When you're here, you're family." "Joey's Life Insurance. We're there when you need us most.") Don't ever clobber it. Just say it. One on one. Easy.

You don't need days to prepare the copy. It's not Chekhov or Stoppard, or even Neil Simon or Joe DiPietro. You can absorb it almost instantly. And, it's never longer than 60 seconds! Most of the time it's 15 seconds. My big secret acting tip for cold-reading commercial copy would be: start with yourself (how you would say the words), hook into the feeling, look it over a time or two, and deliver it as naturally as you possibly can.

Also, always know that no one else will deliver the copy the way you will. Your uniqueness is what will cut through; which is why when you approach it by starting with yourself and you bring your own honest emotions to it, your read will pop. It won't be stilted or phony or pushed. It'll just be you.

One more word: sometimes actors are asked to read cold at a TV or film audition. Not often, but I've been in circumstances where I went into read for one character and the casting director says, "Why don't you take a look at Cop No. 2 as well." In those situations, I often use my big secret acting tip (see above) that I use at commercial auditions. Because you can't go wrong (especially in film) if you start with yourself and remain simple, honest, and real. Break a leg.

James Brochitta, actor

Chapter 17

10 TIPS FOR COLD READING DAYTIME TV SHOWS

I look for someone who makes strong choices. I generally audition people for under-five's, but also for extra work. I want to see if the actor makes the character his own. I don't care if an actor makes a bad strong choice, as long as it's a strong choice. Even a bad strong choice allows me to see what you are capable of doing. It's easier for me to say "Pull back" then it is to say "Pump it up." If I know someone has the energy and capability to do it, then I trust you more that you'll do well on the set.

Lamont Craig, casting director,
As the World Turns

1. Again, all the rules of cold reading apply to auditioning for daytime television. Determine the given circumstances in the scene:

   • What is this scene about?

   • Who is the character?

   • Where is the character?

   • What time of day or night is it?

   • What is the character doing in the scene?

- What does he want (the intention), and what is preventing him (objective) from getting it? Knowing (and playing) the intention and finding (and playing) the conflict is crucial to any scene.

2. It's helpful if you are familiar with the story line of the show. It will help you in your audition if you have some sense where your character fits into the ongoing plot.

3. You always want to keep the read conversational. You want to make your delivery as real as possible. Talk as "you": try not to be too theatrical in the audition.

4. Whoever you read with (the casting director, a reader, or another actor), maintain a natural (not locked) eye contact.

5. The more immediate you can make the read, the more successful you'll be in the audition.

6. Make it personal, using your honest feelings in this imaginary situation.

7. There is an intensity in the acting in daytime. The characters love or hate very deeply. When auditioning for daytime, you want to discover what they want and play it fully, honestly, and with conviction.

8. You need to decide what the scene is about and be able to tell that story in your audition.

9. If the character is described as "very sexy," don't just play sexy. Decide what makes him or her sexy and see if you can find that place in you.

10. Never audition for a role on daytime television (or any role) unless you are willing to commit to the job if you get it.

Chapter 18

INTERVIEWS WITH CASTING DIRECTORS OF DAYTIME TV SHOWS

Rob Decina (RD), casting director, *Guiding Light,* **author of**
  The Art of Auditioning

Mary Clay Boland (MB), casting director, *As the World Turns*

Fran Bascom (FB), casting director, *Days of Our Lives*

Mark Teschner (MT), casting director, *General Hospital*

1. What things do you think actors should be looking for when reading the sides for the first time?

RD: Actors should be looking to identify the character's thoughts and feelings. In a cold reading, my expectations are not very demanding. I think it is essential that the actor try and understand and then express the thoughts and feelings that the characters are dealing with in the scene as clearly and naturally as possible.

MB: The first thing an actor should do when getting sides for daytime, prime time, or theater is to figure out the objective of the scene. What does your character want?

FB: It depends on what kind of role. For a U/5 [under five], it's helpful to recognize whether the role is there mostly for exposition, which occurs more often than not, or whether there is some more meaningful interaction. For a U/5, this would be necessarily limited, but for a day player role, it could be comic relief, or possibly a kind of public service message. For a recurring role, there would normally be some kind of relationship with one of the contract roles (employee, henchman, and so on). On Days of Our Lives, our contract roles usually involve a recast, or bear some relationship to one of our existing characters, so some familiarity with the show is essential and would go a long way to making sense out of sides for a contract role.

MT: When an actor gets sides for the first time they should get sense of what the relationship is between the two characters in the scene, and then what the objective is in the scene. Although that sounds basic, it is crucial. An actor needs to make strong, truthful choices that bring the scene to life.

2. Any advice on cold readings that you feel may be helpful for actors auditioning for you?

RD: Make it about the now. The immediacy of the moment is important. Don't get bogged down in back-story and subtext. Don't worry about what happens next. Make it about the pages in your hand.

MB: I have to be honest. I do not give cold readings very often. They are a good test to see if an actor can quickly make choices about a scene and to see how quickly they can memorize the material, but I find it best to give an actor at least a day with the sides. I am usually casting series regular roles, and I want people to come in as prepared as possible.

Now, for day-player roles, I do give cold sides. I can tell right away if the person is a trained actor by how long he needs with the scene and how well he works with the sides after a short amount of time. If you are good with cold readings, chances are you will be able to handle the rapid pace of daytime television.

FB: We don't often do cold readings per se. We typically send the sides to actors well before the reading, at least a day for U/5's [under fives] or principal roles. But on the odd occasion when we ask someone to read on the spur of the moment, we always take that fact into consideration. Furthermore, since soaps work so fast and have to tell a story so quickly, often it is not the actor's performance that matters most but a look or a type of personality that "reads" immediately. It goes without saying this has to be backed up by plenty of training and experience, preferably in theater.

MT: Again, an actor needs to come in with a point of view about what the scene is about and who the character is that he is reading for. Even in a cold reading where the actor might not have a lot of time with the material, it is essential to find a way to bring the scene to life.

3. Specifically, what do you expect from an actor at your auditions?

RD: It's simple: I expect that the actors have worked on the sides. I expect that they have made choices about the character, the relationship, and the story. I expect them to display those choices.

MB: I expect every actor to come prepared. They should be dressed nicely and be prepared with the scene. Every actor should come in with choices already made. You should also be able to make adjustments quickly if the casting director has a note for you.

FB: When you ask about auditions, I take that to mean callbacks for contract roles. In those cases, we expect the actors to have worked on the scene with a coach wherever possible, particularly given the fact that most of our contract roles go to very young actors who may not be completely comfortable with the process of interpreting the beats of soap opera material.

MT: I expect the things I mentioned in questions 1 and 2. An actor needs to be prepared and make choices. I am looking for an actor who is truthful in the work and has a sense of who he is.

4. What do you feel are the biggest mistakes actors make at auditions?

RD: I think the biggest mistakes actors make are not being prepared enough. They glance at the material and hope for something special to happen in the audition. When actors do that, they are putting too much trust in the reader and the evaluators (casting director, writer, director). Actors need to learn that it is their audition; their choices and the playing of those choices will determine the success, or lack there of, of the audition opportunity.

MB: I do *not* like it when an actor comes in with excuses: "I just got this scene" "I had a photo shoot and could not look at the scene until now." Do not waste my time or yours by coming in unprepared. Every audition is essentially a job interview. You would never go in for a job interview at a bank disheveled and fresh out of bed saying you had to work all night in a bar and were unable to get up on time. It is important to be professional.

FR: Bringing props into auditions, especially callbacks for the producers, is a definite don't. Also, drastically changing your look between the initial reading and the callback is not a good idea, although we try to be understanding if the three-day beard is for a part that works tomorrow. But, for goodness sake, don't shave your head on a whim right before an audition.

MT: The biggest mistakes are actors who come in with no point of view about the scene or the character. I am looking for that special actor who brings a scene to life and puts his mark on the role. It is an unusually competitive business. For a contract role, I audition two hundred to three hundred actors—so an actor really has to be on top of his game to stand out.

5. If you had one piece of advice to offer actors regarding auditioning for daytime television, what would it be?

RD: Do not treat it like a "daytime audition." Do not get fooled into thinking that because it is a daytime scene that the acting has to be different. I have never directed an actor to do a scene more appropriate to soaps. Acting is acting, and I am always looking for good acting no matter the genre.

MB: I hate to narrow it down to daytime because this is true for any type of audition you are going in for. Come prepared, look the part. By this I mean, if it is a professional role, wear something appropriate. If it is more of a blue-collar role, keep that in mind. This does *not* mean to wear costumes. That is entirely unnecessary. Yet if you are coming in for a lawyer role, it may be a good idea to wear a collared shirt and nice pants instead of jeans and a T-shirt. This is perhaps the most important thing to remember. Only come in for a project if you want to do the role and are available for the project. There is nothing more annoying than an actor who comes in repeatedly for a role and then informs us that he is not available for those specific dates. That is extremely frustrating and can give a permanent bad impression to the executive producers and network.

FB: Watch the show or at the very least visit the show's website to find out the basics of the show's characters and at least some familiarity with the inevitably Byzantine nature of the relationships therein.

MT: Daytime auditioning is no different from other auditioning. We are looking for talented actors.

EPILOGUE

Welcome to the end of my book. I hope you've learned something from the previous pages and enjoyed yourself along the way. I realize that there is a lot of information in this book. The more you can retain for your cold-reading auditions, the better. Rereading the book every once in a while will help you remember many of the things you want to include at your next cold-reading (or any) audition.

Perhaps you've noticed that there is some information in the book that's been repeated (and often). I did this so you'd realize that when it comes to cold readings, no matter whether for theater, film, or TV commercials, certain rules come into play to be successful. Once you've learned to make these rules a part of your cold-reading audition, you'll have (if you have the talent) successful audition experiences and start booking more often.

Utilizing and personalizing the given circumstances of all material is key to winning auditioning. Yes, those basics that you learned in your acting classes are the key element to winning cold-reading (and all) auditions.

Knowing how to enter and leave the audition room is more important than you likely realized. I know of several casting directors who swear they can tell within the first fifteen seconds whether or not they'll give an actor a callback—before the actor even opens his mouth. A lot of it has to do with the energy you bring into the room, as well as how you carry yourself.

Preparation in the waiting area can make or break an audition for an actor. I've worked with many actors who made great choices for their audition, only to sabotage their work by not preparing correctly. That prebeat before you say your first word can be the launchpad to a callback. Hoping you can "get into it" and wing it is not the way to audition. The casting director may have a small attention span. If you're not there at the top of your audition, you may not have his attention by the end. You'll have lost him by the second or third line.

Hopefully I've impressed you with how important the other character is in your scene. Even if you have the worst actor reading opposite you at an audition, you can still impress the auditors. Again, much of this depends on an understanding of the material and the choices that you've made. Walking into an audition without having made strong, personalized choices is like walking into a room with no clothes on; you can't fake it.

And finally, remember that acting should be a pleasurable experience, not a stressful and tortuous one. Making believe should be fun. If you really want to learn the secret to acting, watch little children play. Their focus and concentration could put some actors to shame.

Try to enjoy your auditions. The more fun you can have, the less angst you'll feel, and the more successful you'll be. Think of each audition as an adventure, an opportunity to perform. It's also a great way to meet new casting directors, actors, and writers.

I sincerely wish you all the best of luck in your career. I hope that this book has been helpful.

RECOMMENDED BOOKS

Alterman, Glenn. *The Perfect Audition Monologue*. Smith and Kraus, 2003.

Beard, Jocelyn A. *222 Monologues, 2 Minutes and Under*. Smith and Kraus, 1997.

Berland, Terry, and Deborah Quellette. *Breaking into Commercials*. Penguin Books, 1997.

Friedman, Ginger Howard. *The Perfect Monologue: How to Find and Perform the Monologue That Will Get You the Part*. Limelight Editions, 1990.

Haber, Margie, with Barbara Babchick. *How to Get the Part Without Falling Apart*. Lone Eagle, Watson-Guptill Publications, 1999.

Harper, Angel. *Angel Harper's Master the Art of Cold Reading*. Heaven Sent Publishing, 2003.

Hooks, Ed. *The Audition Book*. Backstage Books, Watson-Guptill Publications, 1996.

Hunt, Gordon. *How to Audition for TV, Movies, Commercials, Plays, Musicals*. Harper and Row, 1977.

Jory, Jon. *Tips: Ideas for Actors*. Smith and Kraus, 2000.

Kanner, Eliem and Denny Martin Flinn. *How Not to Audition*. Lone Eagle, 2003.

Kohlhaas, Karen, *The Monologue Audition: A Practical Guide for Actors*. Limelight Editions, 2002.

Logan, Tom. *Acting in the Million Dollar Minute*. Limelight Editions, 2005.

Merlin, Joanna. *Auditioning: An Actor Friendly Guide*. Vantage Books, 2001.

Shepard, John W. *Auditioning and Acting for the Camera*. Smith and Kraus, 2004.

PERMISSIONS

SEAGULLS ON SULLIVAN STREET by Anastasia Traina. Contact Julianne Hausler at New York office, (212) 545-9895.

HARDBALL by Michael Bettencourt, Robert E. Ozasky, and Dean B. Kaner. Copyright © Dean B. Kaner and Michael Bettencourt.

THE DEAD BOY by Joe Pintauro. Contact David Williams at Mojaveartistmanagement@Cox.net.

GOD'S GAME by Lanie Robertson. For permission to perform, contact Rosenstone/Wender, 38 East 29th Street, New York, NY 10016, (212) 795-9445.

I'M BREATHING THE WATER NOW by Bashore Halow. Copyright by Bashore Halow. Reprinted by permission of the author. Rights available through the author. Email: Bhalow@ yahoo.com.

BAD REPUTATION by Penny Arcade. For permission to perform write to www.pennyarcade.tv *or* www.myspace.com/penny arcadeny. Reprinted by permission of the author.

NEW YORK VALUES by Penny Arcade. For permission to perform write to www.pennyarcade.tv *or* www.myspace.com/penny arcadeny. Reprinted by permission of the author.

SMITH AND KRAUS AUDITIONING BOOKS

AUDITION TECHNIQUE

Hot Tips for Cold Readings: Some Do's and Don'ts for Actors at
Auditions By Nina Finburgh Illust. by Anne McArthur

Loving to Audition: The Audition Workbook by Larry Silverberg

Scenes I've Seen: A Casting Director's Original Scenes
and Interpretive Notes by Dorian Dunas

FINDING A MONOLOGUE

The Perfect Audition Monologue by Glenn Alterman

The Ultimate Monologue Index, 2nd Edition Ed. by Karen Morris

AUDITIONING FOR MUSICAL THEATER

How to Audition for the Musical Theater by Donald Oliver

How to Audition for the Musical Theater II: Finding the Song
by Stuart Ostrow

AUDITIONING FOR FILM AND TELEVISION

Auditioning and Acting for the Camera: Proven Techniques for
Auditioning and Performing in Film, Episodic TV, Sit-Coms, Soap Operas,
Commercials, and Industrials by John Shepard

The Camera Smart Actor by Richard Brestoff

For more information, to order, or to download our complete catalogue,
visit www.smithandkraus.com. Or call toll-free (888) 282-2881.